The FOOD TRUCK HANDBOOK

D0047141

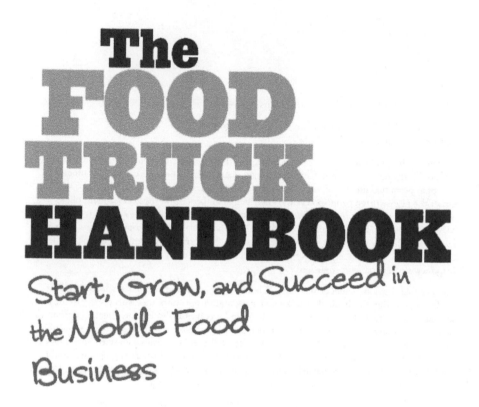

The FOOD TRUCK HANDBOOK

Start, Grow, and Succeed in the Mobile Food Business

DAVID WEBER

WILEY

John Wiley & Sons, Inc.

Published by John Wiley & Sons, Inc., Hoboken, New Jersey.
Published simultaneously in Canada.

For general information on our other products and services or for technical support, please contact our Customer Care Department within the United States at (800) 762-2974, outside the United States at (317) 572-3993 or fax (317) 572-4002.

Wiley publishes in a variety of print and electronic formats and by print-on-demand. Some material included with standard print versions of this book may not be included in e-books or in print-on-demand. If this book refers to media such as a CD or DVD that is not included in the version you purchased, you may download this material at http://booksupport.wiley.com. For more information about Wiley products, visit www.wiley.com.

Library of Congress Cataloging-in-Publication Data:

Weber, David, 1977-
    The food truck handbook: start, grow, and succeed in the mobile food business / David Weber.
      p. cm.
    Includes index.
    ISBN: 978-1-118-20881-6 (pbk); ISBN: 978-1-118-22867-8 (ebk);
    ISBN: 978-1-118-24118-9 (ebk); ISBN: 978-1-118-26595-6 (ebk)
      1. Food industry and trade—United States—Management. 2. Food service—
United States—Management. 3. New business enterprises—United States. I. Title.
HD9005.W38 2012
647.95—dc23

          2012004740

Printed in the United States of America

V10010668_053019

For Juliet

Contents

Foreword

MOBILE VENDING has seen a monumental shift in the past three years. What was an underground and unseen industry has become one of the fastest growing trends in food service. I have tried to do my part in advocating for the industry both in Los Angeles and on the national scene. However, mobile vending and the advocacy that supports it must be done locally. David Weber has been exceedingly good at running a successful food truck business while diligently advocating for the rights of all mobile vendors in the largest city in the United States. David's solid restaurant background and inventive style is the reason for Rickshaw Dumpling Truck's success. Even in one of the most competitive cities in the United States, the Rickshaw Dumpling Truck continues to be a leader in the industry both in quality and business practice. David is also the founder of the New York City Food Truck Association (NYCFTA), an advocacy organization that has led the charge against unfair and overly restrictive regulations. Juggling his time between running a successful food truck business and an advocacy organization in the largest US market makes David one of the premier experts in the food truck field.

The new food truck industry is suffering from a lack of resources when it comes to the new gourmet food truck trend. This book will help prospective mobile vendors understand what it takes to start a mobile food business that will get the attention of customers, turn a profit, and stand the test of time. A large part of running a successful food truck is being able to serve a desirable product quickly while still making a profit. David's experience with food service in both restaurants and food trucks provides the reader with real world service solutions for day-to-day food truck operations. These solutions are imperative for running a successful food truck business.

Starting a food truck business is no small feat. Menu selection, truck wrap design, cost outs, market research, and dealing with the various regulations all seem daunting to the new food truck operator. A common complaint from veteran food truck operators is that there were no resources available to them before they first launched. Much of their day-to-day operations in the first few months were learning the business on the go. This lack of resources led to a high failure rate in some areas of the country, especially in the more competitive cities. Prospective mobile vendors will find this book a wellspring of information in a new industry with very few resources. The step-by-step layout takes mobile vendors through issues that they will have to deal with while launching their trucks and through the life of their businesses.

As the mobile food industry grows, it is imperative that the resources that support it can provide accurate and up-to-date information about the issues that will have an effect on all vendors. This book takes a step in the right direction by laying the groundwork for a more professional industry. A more professional industry will lead to more respect for vendors and more legitimacy for the industry as a whole. The strong following from customers will continue to extend to local communities if the industry continues to grow responsibly and professionally.

—**Matthew Geller**
Chief Executive Officer
Southern California Mobile Food Vendors' Association
(SoCalMFVA)

Preface

I FIRST discovered the enormous, life-changing power of entrepreneurship 1,000 kilometers east of Madagascar in the middle of the Indian Ocean. I spent the summer of 2003 in Mauritius, working as a consultant for the World Bank and assessing potential technology investments to support local businesses. I was meant to help five women entrepreneurs with their businesses, but they ended up helping me discover the transformative power of entrepreneurship.

I was amazed at the resourcefulness, ingenuity, and passion of these women. While most of them had started with very little, each of them had become an expert in her field. One woman manufactured stuffed animals for export to Germany; another ran a manufacturing company that sold clothes to France; one had a gourmet food company that made all-natural honeys and jams that were favored by the prince of Morocco; another ran a tourism company that brought visitors to Mauritius from India; and the last had a furniture manufacturing plant. Each of them had taken a risk to open her own business. Each had started small and had grown her business into something larger that was a positive force in her community, family, and personal development.

My experiences in Mauritius lit an entrepreneurial spark in me that I'd like to share with you. The mobile food industry and food trucks, in particular, are exciting because they make entrepreneurship accessible. Everyone has some experience with food, a passion for a special dish, or a family recipe that has been handed down to him or her. However, not everyone has the knowledge or expertise to translate that experience into a successful business. This book is an effort to help build that expertise and make the mobile food industry even more accessible.

I've spent the past five years obsessing on the critical success factors in starting and growing mobile food businesses. In addition to running a business that operates four food trucks in one of the most competitive hospitality markets in the United States, I've also worked as an advocate to improve the industry to provide safe, healthy choices for consumers, growth opportunity for hospitality professionals, revenue for local government, and a fair market for the local hospitality industry.

This book concisely summarizes much of what I've learned and offers practical advice to aspiring entrepreneurs on thoroughly thinking through what it is to own and operate a food truck.

While a truck seems like a much more manageable undertaking than a restaurant, the strict constraints on size mean that each decision made about the design or operation matters more. Consequently, it is extremely important to plan ahead. If you don't fully consider small details as you're planning your operation, the consequences can cause a lot of problems in the future. And while operating a food truck can be extremely rewarding in a number of ways, food truck operations are often romanticized by the media. This book aims to cut through much of the hype about the industry and offers an accurate portrayal of life on the street so that potential entrepreneurs can make informed decisions about jumping into the industry.

My goal is to provide a rigorous foundation in the details you'll most need to consider when planning and operating a food truck business. The book touches on a wide variety of issues, from choosing a concept; to developing a business plan; to picking a vehicle; and to designing the build, branding, marketing, purchasing, hiring, and management strategies for mobile trucks. While this book is aimed at an aspiring food truck entrepreneur, there are lessons to be learned both by mobile food novices and professionals. The book offers food truck fans "insider" info on the *real* life of food truck operators and provides individuals inside and outside of the food industry with important business advice and insight.

The book is organized into four major sections: Plan, Start, Succeed, and Grow.

1. **Plan:** This section examines the research and planning that is required before opening a food truck. Chapters focus on key aspects of a mobile food business, such as local regulations, menu, format, branding, and finances, all of which will ultimately be incorporated into the business plan.
2. **Start:** This section walks you through some of the key decisions you'll need to make as you are building your first food truck. Chapters highlight truck procurement, kitchen layout, menu design, and choosing vending locations.
3. **Succeed:** This section walks you through important areas to focus on to ensure that your truck is being run as effectively as possible. Chapters discuss efficient operations, the importance of brand, and the ways in which food trucks can connect with customers. Special emphasis is given to the role of social media.
4. **Grow:** This section discusses ways to scale and grow a mobile food business. Food truck entrepreneurs have successfully grown their businesses from one truck to multiple trucks. Other options explored are brick-and-mortar restaurants, wholesaling, and franchising.

Interwoven throughout is a series of interviews to provide some advice directly from operators working on the streets, who share their thoughts on each of the particular issues that pertain to food truck operations.

Writing this book was both thrilling and daunting. The one thing that kept me going was the confidence that it might help you succeed with your entrepreneurial endeavors.

I hope that this book helps you to pave your path toward becoming a successful entrepreneur.

—**David Weber**

Acknowledgments

THIS BOOK could not have been written without the help and support of a great number of people.

First, I'd like to thank my business partner, Kenny Lao. The more I wrote, the more I realized how much insight into the hospitality industry I gleaned by working with Kenny. Moreover, without his flexibility and efforts, as well as the contributions of Thor, Carrie, Daniel, Monica, Tom, Letica, and the whole Rickshaw team, I would have never found the time to get this book written. Thank you for keeping the operation organized and running smoothly.

Matthew Geller of the Southern California Mobile Food Vendors' Association (SoCalMFVA) is doing great work on behalf of the food truck industry across the country. Thank you for your time, assistance, and collaboration in our shared advocacy efforts to improve the future of this growing industry.

Special thanks go to Ari Ginsberg, Derek Kaye, and Tim Volkema, who each took the time to review the book and provided feedback and inspiration that greatly improved the final product.

Susan Povich, Derek Kaye, and Hiassam Atwi all provided invaluable assistance both in sharing their insights and experiences in the food truck industry with me, as well as managing and growing the NYC Food Truck Association. I also thank all the busy entrepreneurs who took time out of their schedules to be interviewed for this book, including Natasha Case of Coolhaus, Thomas DeGeest of

Wafels & Dinges, Richard Kallman of CupcakeStop, Keith Klein of Milk Truck NYC, Kenny Lao of Rickshaw Dumplings, Jen Lyon of MeanRed Productions, Randy Miller of MobiMunch, Laura O'Neill of Van Leeuwen Artisan Ice Cream, Susan Povich of Red Hook Lobster Pound, Alex Rein of Kelvin Natural Slush Co., and David Shapiro of Taïm Mobile.

Nick Marsh and Michael Bonadies have been great mentors and have provided me with tremendous advice and counsel over the years. Thank you for your guidance and thoughts on the hospitality industry.

Many thanks to Lucy Schaeffer (lucyschaeffer.com) for her stunning photography and for always making our food, not to mention me, look good.

Many of the interviews and other background details of the food truck industry are based on the contributions of a trio of resourceful researchers: Lucas Adams, Alecia Eberhardt, and Julia Kayser.

Thank you to my family, in particular my wife, Juliet, my parents, Mike and Kathy Weber, and my brother, Jon Weber, for being both sounding boards and sources of support throughout my career as an entrepreneur, and, in particular, throughout the process of writing this book.

I have great appreciation for the grounding in business studies I received at the New York University Stern School of Business. In particular, I'd like to mention Professor Sally Blount-Lyon. You were right: learning how to manage others is more important than any other skill in managing small businesses.

Last, but not least, thanks are due to dessertbaby.com for the amazing cookies that powered me through the final stretch of writing this book.

Introduction

THE FOOD TRUCK phenomenon has taken the country by storm. From New York to Los Angeles, the number, the variety, and the quality of food trucks are on the rise. In 2011, the mobile food industry in the United States was estimated to be at $630 million.[1] I think this sum dramatically underestimates the size of the industry. I believe that the mobile food industry in New York City alone is at least $450 million. The National Restaurant Association stated in 2011 that food trucks are the *single fastest growing sector* of the restaurant industry.[3]

If you have any doubts, you can see this for yourself on the streets. Fans are queuing up across the country for tasty food from local trucks. According to an American Express survey, the percentage of respondents that had visited a food truck doubled from 13 percent in August 2009 to 26 percent in July 2010.[4]

From Food Network's *The Great Food Truck Race* (a cross-country food truck trek) to the Cooking Channel's *Eat Street*, media coverage on popular television shows reflects the food truck phenomenon. Zagat's inclusion of food truck for the first time in its 2011 *New York City Restaurants* guide has helped make food trucks an integral part of contemporary city life.

Food Truck Fundamentals

The food truck industry has grown rapidly, from 2007 to the present, while the hospitality industry in general has been flagging in the weak economic environment. The rise of the food truck in the public's imagination is driven by a number of factors including:

- The economic downturn made capital more scarce and the low start-up costs of a food truck more tempting.
- Developments in social media make it easier to track trucks over space and time and have expanded their appeal to broader audiences.
- Relatively rapid improvement can be found in the overall quality and variety of foods now served on trucks.
- The predominant factor, however, may be that customers are looking for more value for their food dollar. Limited by the constraints of operating out of a limited space, today's food truck entrepreneurs are almost exclusively specialists. They do one thing, and they do it very, very well. The limited overhead keeps costs down, and by focusing on a few menu items, food truck operators can focus on getting good pricing and delivering high-quality food for just a few items, which often results in a product that is above average in quality and below average in price.

Food Truck History

Mobile vendors date back hundreds of years and were present with the growth of most major urban or trade areas throughout the United States. These include what we would consider today to be "pushcarts" or "food carts" that sell premade items.[5]

1690s: In New York City, street food dates back to 1691, emerging with the entrance of Dutch settlers.[6]

1860s: American "chuck wagons" emerged to feed cattle hands crossing the United States in the late 1860s and early 1870s. These chuck wagons were created by Colonel Charles Goodnight, who ran the Goodnight-Loving Trail, a cattle drive in Texas. He needed a way to feed his cowboys on the long drive and the "mobile kitchen" was created.[7,8,9]

1870s: As far back as the 1870s, *tamaleros* (tamale carts) were extremely popular in Los Angeles, and by 1901 more than 100 tamale wagons roamed LA, some even creating mobile kitchens by tapping into city gas and water lines. These wagons were the precursor to the *lonchero*, or the "taco truck," which dominated Los Angeles for most of the twentieth century.

What is thought to be the first traditional "food truck," similar to what we see now, was opened by Walter Scott in Providence, RI in 1872. His wagon sold breakfast sandwiches and pies to workers at nearby establishments. Charles Palmer patented the "lunch wagon" design in 1891.[10]

1900s: By the early 1900s, food carts and "mobile vendors" were extremely popular, with thousands estimated to have worked the streets of New York. It is thought that the rise in street carts around this time was due to the rise in people working outside the home (i.e., not in agriculture) and the growth of urban environments. Food carts and wagons also began operating at night in bigger cities (Boston, New York) to accommodate the nightlife of those going to the theater.[11]

Lunch wagons transformed into food trucks with advances in technology. In the early 1900s to the 1930s, street vendors (trucks and carts) in New York were subject to many regulations, but these typically were not enforced in the immigrant-saturated areas of the city. Thus, immigrants ran much of the mobile food scene, and the food choices reflected that.[5]

Street food gained a reputation for being both unhealthy and unsanitary, possibly because the horses who pulled the wagons also defecated close by on the streets.[12]

1950s: The association with immigrant culture and unfamiliar ethnic food created a decline in popularity throughout the mid-twentieth century.

The phrase "roach coach" began to be used mid-century to refer to the unsanitary conditions of the trucks. Trucks were associated mainly with blue-collar society, as they tended to serve their cheap lunches around construction sites and military bases.[13]

2000s: The rise of the modern food truck. The declining economy in 2007 and 2008 resulted in fewer construction projects and therefore fewer construction sites and fewer customers for the standard "roach coach" food truck. At the same time, many high-end chefs were out of work and looking for a new way to use their skills. Thus, the "high-end" or "gourmet" food truck came into being.[13]

Recent Food Truck Milestones

2007: Armenco, a food truck manufacturer in Los Angeles, began to shift business from traditional lunch trucks to custom "gourmet" food trucks.[3]

2008: The opening and subsequent success of KogiBBQ in LA, one of the original gourmet trucks, signals the shift in the food truck landscape.[14]

2010: The annual National Restaurant Association (NRA) Show featured mobile food-related exhibitions for the first time.[15]

The Food Network broadcasted their new reality competition show, *The Great Food Truck Race.*[15]

2011: In April another show on the mobile food industry premiered, this time on the Cooking Channel, called *Eat Street* and featured different street foods from across the country.

Zagat added a Food Truck section to their restaurant reviews in some cities.[14]

Culinary schools in some states began to add mobile food cooking classes to their curriculum.[3]

The Future of Food Trucks

Food trucks are far from hitting their peak. The market is still developing, and there are many opportunities for new operators who want to open trucks to sell food that they are passionate about. Technomic, a food industry consulting firm, reported in July 2011 that 91 percent of customers polled believe that food trucks are not a passing fad, but rather a trend with "staying power."[3] Growth in food trucks is driven by two major forces: the growth of a mobile food culture in new municipalities across the United States and the improved access to food that the trucks offer in these markets as well as established markets. Customers appreciate the value and quality of mobile food and will continue to embrace the industry so long as operators deliver clean, tasty, and interesting products at a fair price.

Food trucks are great for cities. They get customers out on the street and create a sense of community. As local municipalities learn the value of what food trucks have to offer in terms of tax revenues, job growth, tourism, activating public space, and fostering entrepreneurship, local regulations will improve. One of the most compelling aspects of food trucks is their ability to act as an incubator for entrepreneurs to start a viable, cash flow–positive business that they can grow into a brick-and-mortar establishment to become a more stable part of the community.

In addition to opportunities for food truck entrepreneurs, there is also a wide variety of opportunities in supporting industries that will develop as the food truck market matures. Food truck operators are looking for better trucks, more eco-friendly power supplies, quieter generators, small-run food manufacturers, more customizable insurance resources, more robust financing tools, marketing partners, and information technology resources.

It is an exciting time for mobile food in America. The industry is big and growing fast. I look forward to seeing what you will bring to the streets.

Plan: Preparing for Success

WHILE PLANNING ISN'T the most exciting thing in the world, it is an absolute necessity before jumping into the mobile food-vending industry. Right now, there is a lot of dynamism and energy in the industry, which makes it exciting and attractive, but it is also extremely chaotic. Regulations, competitors, and vending locations are changing daily. The following chapters will help give you the foundation of knowledge and expertise you need to form the initial shape of your business and develop a robust plan to help make the food truck of your dreams a reality.

Is the Trucker's Life for Me?

I GET ABOUT three to four e-mails a day from people looking to open food trucks. People who are passionate about food and weighed down by the routine of an office job are often attracted to the promise of freedom that owning a food truck seems to convey. While the experience of eating at a brightly colored and well-designed food truck is fun, and the concept of owning a food truck looks like a carefree way to cruise around the city and make a lot of cash on a sunny day, the reality is much different. There are some amazing advantages to operating a food truck, but also some big challenges. It is definitely an exciting opportunity, but it is good to embrace this lifestyle with a complete knowledge of the pros and cons of this career.

A Day in the Life

In order to get a better sense of what life is like as a food truck operator, I thought I'd share with you a typical day. Food truck entrepreneurs often work on their trucks on a daily or near-daily basis. Some entrepreneurs aspire to grow their businesses and move out of the daily operations as they build a fleet of trucks or settle into a brick-and-mortar establishment. It helps to begin with the end in mind, but regardless of your goals, you'll definitely be spending a lot of time on your truck.

The length of a typical day can vary, depending on the type of food you serve. To service just the lunch shift could easily require a 10-hour day, from 8 AM to 6 PM, including prep and end-of-day cleaning. To make ends meet, some trucks run breakfast, lunch, and dinner, with load-in starting at 4 AM and not ending until 2 AM.

9

In this example, let's assume that you are a savory food truck serving the lunch crowd.

At the Commissary

The day begins at the commissary. It's the home of your truck, your tools, and your food: everything you need to run the operation. Your commissary is probably in an industrial district outside of town, where the rent is cheaper. Because it is an out-of-the-way location, the commute may be inconvenient for you and your employees.

You'll need to arrive at the commissary two to four hours before you plan to serve, depending on where your food is prepared, the length of your commute, and traffic in your city. If you're hoping to serve lunch at 11 AM, your team will likely have to be at the commissary by 8 AM at the latest to have enough time to prep, and you'll likely want to arrive before that to get administrative work done before the beginning of the day.

Once there, the first thing you'll need to do is prep any food that you'll be bringing that day. Food trucks generally have small kitchens, so anything you can do ahead of time that can speed up your service and allow you to carry more should be done before you hit the road. You might spend some time making special sauces, cutting vegetables, or baking cookies. The time you spend prepping really depends on the type of truck. It could be a few minutes of assembling a hot sauce or hours of slowly braising barbecued ribs. Many trucks employ a prep team that just prepares food.

Once your food is in order, you need to check out the truck and see if it's ready for the day's shift. You run through a checklist to ensure that nothing unexpected has happened overnight. You check that the truck is plugged in and that any refrigeration units onboard have been working, and you also check for any food that might have spoiled.

You'll need to consider the location where you'll be going for the day and what the sales might be before you load up. No use bringing food you cannot sell, because it will go bad and cost you money. At the same time, you don't want to bring too little, because you'll miss out on potential sales. Pull everything onboard as quickly as you can. It helps if you have an employee so you can divide the work: someone grabs supplies while the other stows them. Because you've been doing this for weeks it goes quickly: You refill all the essentials first, fresh water, ice, and propane. Cold products go in the coolers, frozen products go in the freezer, dry products get stowed in cabinets, and paper products are refilled.

It's time to head out. Check the fuel gauge and don't forget to unplug the truck before you pull out.

Setting Up on the Street

Some days you can breeze directly to your vending location, but other times it can take hours. Most trucks have a set of spots that they frequent, be it on the street, in food truck lots, or in private properties.

If you are vending on the street, allow extra time in your morning routine. Vending on the street is hard, because you need to find a place for your truck to vend daily. In any city, there is always a lot of competition for street parking, but there is even more competition for good street-vending locations. Often, a number of trucks might be vying for the same spot, which can cause conflict. It is extremely bad form to roll up on another vendor's established spot and can lead to conflict that can escalate very quickly. There are all sorts of examples of physical violence between vendors. Don't let this be you. If you cannot find your first choice, keep looking. If time is running low until lunch, you'll have to gamble and drive to other spots you use during the rest of the week. In the worst-case scenario, the whole day can be lost due to lack of a parking spot, so it is important to scout a number of possible vending spots in advance.

Once you're parked, it's prep time. Hopefully, you found a spot by 10 AM, which will give you an hour to prep before lunch. Turn off the truck, turn on the generator, and start heating up your equipment. Make sure to count the cash in the register before the start of the shift, and be ready to run to the bank if you need smaller bills.

Before opening your awning, run one last check to make sure every machine is running and all your food is fresh and ready to serve. Once you have a first batch of food ready, you're ready to serve.

Open for Business

By 11 AM you should be ready to open and begin serving your customers. Once open, you have to be ready for anything. Get a rhythm going between you and your partner. Know who is working the register, and who is prepping the food. Be ready to improvise if the situation arises. All kinds of problems can, and will, flare up during your shift.

It's not hard to fall behind on orders, have machines malfunction, run out of smaller bills and have to run to the bank, and encounter other unforeseen dilemmas. All of these are problems that are easily dealt with, as long as you and your team keep your cool.

Once the lunch rush is over and the shift starts winding down around 3 PM, it's time to clean up. Even while you are waiting on the last few customers, start wiping down and cleaning everything up. Once everything is organized and packed away, head back to the commissary, stopping for gas if the truck needs a refill.

Closing

The lunch crowd winds down by 3 PM, so try to make it back to the commissary around 5 PM so that you are not caught in rush-hour traffic. At the commissary, drain all the wastewater into an approved drain and discard all your trash. Then do a thorough cleaning of the truck. Scrub the floors and the walls. Be sure to leave a note for yourself about what food has been left on the truck to save you or your partner some time the next morning. Plug the truck in for the night to keep the fridges running, and you're good until the next shift.

The Best Parts of Operating a Truck

Food truck entrepreneurs come from all walks of life and open trucks for a number of different reasons. Here are some of the best aspects of being in the food truck business.

Happy Customers!

There is nothing like the thrill you'll get from a customer who leaves the truck happy, having eaten a dish that you've made. Satisfied guests are the best.

Personal Expression

Owning a food truck allows you to express your culinary creativity and have control over every aspect of the business, so you can run it the way you want to. If you care deeply about the environment, you can run it environmentally responsibly, or if you care deeply about locally sourced ingredients, you can buy only local food. It's your truck, your rules.

Building a Brand

Food trucks are an ideal platform to build a brand. If you have an idea for a concept that you think could be a great restaurant chain, but you do not have the resources or funding to build out a brick-and-mortar restaurant, a food truck could be the way to go. For a lot less capital, you can get a proof of concept and demonstrate to potential investors that there is demand for your idea and that it would translate well into a restaurant. If you already have an existing restaurant, a food truck is a great way to extend the brand and reach new customers.

Get Out of the Cubicle!

If the movie *Office Space* were written today, you could be sure that the protagonist, Peter Gibbons (played by Ron Livingston), would open his own food truck, rather than getting a job in construction. Food trucks offer the promise of freedom and flexibility, getting you away from the nine-to-five office doldrums and from the administrative challenges and protocols that come with working in a big company. Food trucks are outdoors and mobile. If things aren't working out well, you can always move along to the next great opportunity.

Accessible Entrepreneurship

Running your own business has all sorts of emotional and psychological perks. You will have control over your own schedule. You will have the ability to be involved in every aspect of your business and can make your own arrangements concerning who you do business with. And you'll also have the satisfaction of creating jobs for other people.

The Worst Parts of Operating a Truck

While trucks might look bright and shiny and fun, owning a truck isn't all excitement and smiles. There is a lot of blood, sweat, and tears that go into a successful food truck operation (and even more blood, sweat, and tears can be caused by an unsuccessful food truck operation).

The Tip of the Iceberg

The busy lunch shift for a popular food truck is just a fraction of the operation. Prior to the great two hours of sales that a customer witnesses from noon to 2 PM are hours of training, preparation, lifting, cleaning, and transportation. One thing that cannot be stressed enough is that operating a food truck is extremely hard work. Running a food truck means long days of waking up early to oversee food prep at the commissary in the morning and late nights checking on the cleanliness of the truck after a shift.

Endless Repairs

Food trucks break down *a lot*. And when they break down, everything stops. Besides the cost of these repairs, waiting a week for the fix while you cannot work (and therefore lose income) is unbearably stressful. Add to that the stress of your employees calling and being upset that their shifts have been cancelled and the fact that all the food in the commissary's fridge is going to go bad while your truck is in the shop. Repairs that take down the truck are inevitable and are bad not only for business but also for morale.

Trucks Don't Scale Well

One of the most challenging aspects of food trucks is that the business is not easily scalable. Trucks are generally pretty small operations with one to three people on board at a time. They don't generate enough revenue to support managers, so they require very well-trained and competent employees. Also, because so much of the business is done in cash, "shrinkage" is always a concern. It is very easy for employees to run creative schemes to divert revenue from the legitimate operation into their own pockets.

Conflict

While many consumers love food trucks, they aren't universally appreciated. Unfortunately, conflict with other members of the community can occur, sometimes quite frequently, depending on where you live. Many retail shops, especially restaurant and deli owners, see food trucks only as competitors and not as an opportunity or as collaborators. Also, conflict with other street vendors isn't uncommon. There is often friction between older, more-established street vendors and newer vendors. The best policy is to be cool, be respectful, and stay connected with the community.

Are You a Peddler?

As a food truck entrepreneur, you need to be ready to embrace the life of a peddler, which requires a level of dedication that many underestimate from the onset. The quickest road to success is by operating the truck yourself. The lower revenues of food trucks usually means that they cannot financially support an on-site manager, so as a food truck owner, you are making a full-time commitment to oversee the operations of this business. Being on the truck will also give you the opportunity to define and articulate the brand personally to your customers.

Deal Breakers . . .

There are life's little unhappy accidents that inevitably happen and that can make life on the streets trying, at best.

- **Engine stall:** It can happen at any time: in the middle of a left-hand turn, in the middle of traffic, even while crossing a bridge. It can cause a few moments' delay or shut down a whole shift. Always know where your hand brake is. It can save you from serious trouble.
- **Broken equipment:** If any steamers, cookers, fryers, or freezers are broken, they can ruin an entire shift. Either you're unable to cook anything, or your food has been spoiled.
- **Generator problems:** If the generator doesn't start at all, your shift can be over before it even gets started.

- **Running out of small bills and no bank in sight:** A simple one, but if you don't have small bills, it can impede your ability to sell. No money, no sales. Plan ahead, especially for big events on the weekends.

- **Out of materials:** If you're missing napkins, utensils, or bags, things get especially tough. If you run out of containers for food, you won't be able to sell anything.

- **No parking:** This doesn't seem like a shift-killer, but it can easily stop the day from even starting. If you have to spend most of your time looking for a spot, you'll either miss the lunch rush, be unable to find a spot at all, or open where none of your clientele can find you.

- **Police:** Especially in cities with contention over food trucks, this can be a real problem, depending on the neighborhood. If the police keep forcing you to move, you won't have time to prep or cook, meaning you will not be able to sell during prime meal times and your prospects of earning revenue for the day are ruined.

- **Food spoiled:** If anything has thawed accidently or gone bad, you'll be in trouble. You're either going to be out of an item, or you're going to be hearing some serious complaints from customers.

- **Fender-benders and accidents:** It may or may not be your fault, but a bad enough accident can put your truck out of commission for the foreseeable future.

- **Electrical issues:** Problems with wiring can cause all sorts of problems and lead to overheating, undercooked food, and/or burnouts. In the worst-case scenario, electrical issues could lead to a fire and cause a lot of damage and close your truck for weeks.

- **Propane explosion:** Handle propane extremely carefully. It is very combustible. Never drive with your propane tanks open. If a propane tank is damaged and explodes, it could cause an enormous amount of damage to your staff, your truck, and anyone or anything nearby.

- **Ruining food:** If you're not focused, it's easy to overcook your food. Leaving anything unattended, or forgetting how long you've been cooking it, is a surefire way to do damage to a shift and your reputation. Too many mistakes like this, and you risk running out of food early or not having enough to serve customers on time.

Getting Rich Quick!?

There is money to be made in mobile food, but food trucks are not a get-rich-quick scheme. Food trucks offer lower capital costs, so it is easier to get started as a food truck entrepreneur than as a brick-and-mortar restaurant owner. However, the core economic foundations of the business need to be in place. We will explore the core financial details of operating a food truck in a later chapter. If making a million dollars is your goal, food trucks might not be the best route to achieve your dreams.

Scared?

If this chapter puts some fear into the pit of your stomach, that's okay—it is meant to. Some apprehension is healthy. Opening a food truck business is a major and difficult undertaking, and you should go into it as you would any new venture, with your eyes open to all of the potential hardships and challenges. If you're still optimistic about starting a food truck business, knowing all the challenges that are in store for you, that is a good thing. Now we can move on to the nuts and bolts of planning your business.

Foundations for Success

Success is a slippery word, but in my book, a successful entrepreneur is someone who can build and sustain a viable business.

Beginning with the End in Mind

Every entrepreneur has his or her own ambitions and goals. Some entrepreneurs are looking for a small business where they can support themselves and have the flexibility to work when they want to. Others are looking to start and grow the next fast food chain to sweep the country. Knowing where you want to go will be a big help as you plan your business. You should be able to answer the following things: How big do I want to grow? What do I want to be doing on a daily basis? How much time do I want to put into this business? Where you want to take this business and what you are willing to commit to it has a big impact on the type of business you should develop and how you should operate it.

The Fundamentals: Passion, Cash, and Expertise

While there are a number of things that can contribute to the success of an entrepreneur, the three most important are passion, cash, and expertise.

Passion

Passion is essential because it provides the spark of inspiration that ignites the entire undertaking. Passion is what sustains you during the long, demanding days of street vending. For me, it is the pleasure of watching customers walk away smiling, satisfied with a great meal. Whenever things start to get stressful, I try to get back to what I love and spend an afternoon cashiering and chatting with customers. Passion can also be very important from a marketing perspective. You should think about how your passion for food and hospitality creates a story that ties into the concept of your mobile food business. Compelling stories help you create a brand that customers can relate to and believe in. Passion is the starting point, but passion alone isn't enough to sustain a viable business.

Cash

As they say, "cash is king." Being well capitalized in a new venture is extremely important. Cash gives you time to work out the kinks in your business model and flexibility to make changes if things are going awry. Without a sufficient cash cushion, you are taking a huge gamble in opening a business. There is a reason they call our economic system capitalism. With capital, you can play. Without it, you are out of business. Be smart and raise as much money as you can when times are good and when you have a strong proof of concept. Get a line of credit from your bank: even if you don't need it in the near term, it may prove useful in the long term. The winter could be unseasonably cold. Someone could open a competing truck and take away your business. Having resources to call upon in tough times could make the difference between the success and failure of your business.

Expertise

The number one thing you can do to succeed in this business is to learn as much as you can about it before you start. While many business skills are transferable, it is really how the details are handled that determines the winners and losers in a particular field. The food truck business isn't any different. Knowing how to run a food truck, where to park, how much to prepare each day, where to source ingredients at a fair price, and how to connect with customers comes with time and experience. Buying this book is a good start, but you should be prepared to do your own research and to build your expertise and skill set before set out on your own business.

Building Expertise

At this point, the primary success factor under your control is expertise. Do whatever you can to build your knowledge about business, entrepreneurship, hospitality, and mobile vending.

Get a Job on a Food Truck

If you have the time and the ability, I would strongly encourage you to get a job in the industry. If you haven't worked in hospitality before, get a job in a restaurant or, even better, on a food truck. Be honest with your employers about how you are planning on starting a business someday. Most companies will appreciate your passion and your candor. By working in the industry, you will learn two things: (1) whether a food truck is a good fit for your personality and (2) a lot of the ins and outs of how a hospitality business is run. You'll undoubtedly be thinking of all the ways you could run the business better, and that is great, because hopefully you soon will be putting your ideas to the test! Keep a list. Once you start working on your truck, you'll be so busy you may not have time to deliberate on all the improvements that could be made, so it will be helpful to go back to a time when you were an employee and had less on your plate to examine the business from another perspective.

Read Good Books

When you aren't working on the truck, bone up on business and management skills by reading books on the topic. Here are some books that have provided me with insight into my own business and that I'd recommend you take a look at to get ideas and perspective on how to better run your own venture:

> *The Definitive Book of Body Language* by Allan and Barbara Pease. Dedicated to revealing the "secrets of nonverbal communication," this book provides invaluable insight into interpersonal relationships. Having a strong understanding of body language helps you better judge who to approach on the street and how to do so effectively so that you can build lasting relationships with customers.

The Checklist Manifesto by Atul Gawande. This guide helps you manage and track your daily to-dos. Tracking business protocols on checklists is an important skill to hone, as these lists are integral in keeping your business running smoothly and consistently.

The Death and Life of Great American Cities by Jane Jacobs. Heralded as one of the most influential writers on urban planning in the twentieth century, Jacobs discusses in this book how individuals can provide "eyes on the street" or natural surveillance within a community. This concept is applicable in considering the role food trucks play within society, how they can add to street culture, give back to their neighbors, and improve the life of the community.

Good to Great: Why Some Companies Leap . . . and Others Don't by Jim Collins. A must-read for all business managers that frames the key criteria and discusses the building blocks needed in order to run a successful company and grow it into something larger.

Influence: Science and Practice by Robert Cialdini. An examination of the "psychology of compliance," this book provides useful insight into how to present yourself and how to brand your business in order to connect to customers.

Menu Pricing and Strategy by Jack Miller and David Pavesic. A straightforward guide to how to design a menu, which takes into consideration customer decision making, from creating the layout to assigning price points to organizing content.

Multi-Unit Leadership: The 7 Stages of Building High-Performing Partnerships and Teams by Jim Sullivan. If you plan to grow your mobile food vending business beyond the operation of one truck, this book provides a thorough overview of the core attributes needed to lead and develop a concept into a multi-unit concept or franchise.

Servant Leadership: A Journey into the Nature of Legitimate Power and Greatness by Robert Greenleaf. A highly influential work on management and power, which is grounded in the philosophy that great leaders trust, collaborate, listen, and empower their team for the betterment of both the employee and the larger company.

Setting the Table by Danny Meyer. Specific to the hospitality industry, and a must-read for anyone opening a new food venture, this book provides behind-the-scenes advice and anecdotes that help hospitality professionals tackle the challenges of how to not only meet but consistently exceed customer expectations.

Why Employees Don't Do What They're Supposed to Do and What to Do about It by Ferdinand Fournies. An essential guide to management that provides proven strategies and tactics on how to manage a team and increase employee performance.

Why We Buy: The Science of Shopping by Paco Underhill. A rigorous anthropological study of contemporary consumer culture. This book will help you consider customer perspective and think through where to locate your truck for best business.

Winning by Jack Welch with Suzy Welch. The former CEO of General Electric, Jack Welch provides business leaders with step-by-step advice for succeeding in the corporate world. For food truck operators, I find his chapters on interviewing and hiring particularly useful, especially when screening for higher-level employees.

Track What Is Going on in the Industry

Here are some additional resources that can help you stay abreast of what is happening in the industry.

Cornell Hospitality Quarterly:	hotelschool.cornell.edu/research/chr/pubs
Fast Casual magazine:	fastcasual.com
Harvard Business Review:	hbr.org
Mobile Cuisine magazine:	mobile-cuisine.com
National Restaurant Association:	restaurant.org
Nation's Restaurant News:	nrn.com
QSR magazine:	qsrmagazine.com

Skills and Attributes That Can't Hurt

Personal attributes and skills that lend themselves well to operating a food truck include a ready smile, grace under pressure, customer service skills, culinary know-how, marketing, negotiation, and number crunching.

- **Smiling:** Yes, smiling is that important. Do it. Hire for it.
- **Customer service:** Great customer service is pretty much non-negotiable in the hospitality industry. Connecting with guests is especially important on the street. People who have innate caring and concern for others will do well as truck owners.
- **Culinary know-how:** Since food trucks are in the business of selling food, being able to cook pays off in spades. However, to work well on trucks, great recipes need to be not only tasty but fast to prep and easy to eat on the go. If you aren't comfortable in a commercial kitchen, it might be helpful to take a few cooking classes or hire a consulting chef to get you started.
- **Marketing:** Promotion and marketing savvy is very important. Building a brand 140 characters at a time on Twitter or developing a menu that projects a specific brand identity isn't something that comes naturally to everyone. Some trucks are made on personality alone.
- **Negotiation:** Because so much is often ambiguous on the street, there is a lot of negotiation that will happen on a daily basis, especially with other vendors. Being affable, open-minded, and creative about possible alternatives is very important to finding parking spots.
- **Number crunching:** Even if you aren't a numbers whiz, or maybe especially if you aren't, you should get comfortable with a spreadsheet program, like Microsoft Excel. Spreadsheets can be extremely helpful for managing schedules, calculating breakevens, determining food costs, and all sorts of off-the-cuff calculations that can help you run your business better.
- **Self-knowledge:** Know that you are doing what you want to be doing. Taking the plunge to be an entrepreneur for anyone other than yourself is going to result in problems. Also, be sure to get the support of friends and family. If your spouse resents that you are taking away time from him or her to open your food truck, it is going to be even harder to accomplish your dreams.

Staying Organized

Have a rock-solid method to manage your to-do list. You need to develop something that works for you. Forgetting to do something basic, like changing the oil on your generator, can cost you a lot of time and effort. You'll need a system where to-do list items don't slip through the cracks. My business partner swears by his yellow legal pad, and I prefer to track my to-do list in my iPhone. If you're looking for some advice for how to stay on top, take a look at David Allen's *Getting Things Done*.

Playing by the Rules

BEFORE YOU BUY the step van you've been keeping track of on eBay™, you need to learn all the local laws and regulations that pertain to food truck vending in your hometown. Local regulations play an *essential* role in determining several key elements of your business. Regulations can affect how your truck will be constructed, how you can operate your business, and how you can staff your business. Before you do anything else, you—and every aspiring food truck entrepreneur—should thoroughly research local regulations to make sure that your mobile business is in compliance with the rules and regulations of your local municipality.

When you research local rules, you should be as rigorous as possible. Don't just ask other vendors the rules or look at a summary of the rules online, dig deep into the regulations and read the rules yourself. Go to your local department of health to learn the details of the local regulations for yourself. If there is ambiguity, ask for clarifications in writing. Also, take the time to meet the person in charge of mobile food for the health department and whatever department manages acceptable vending locations for that municipality, be it parks, transportation, or city planning. Having a relationship with a decision maker in these departments will help as you confront future issues or questions about regulations.

If the police ever come to shut you down for violation of a local rule, you're not going to get out of trouble and save the shift by saying, "My friend on the taco truck said it was okay," or "Mary down at City Hall thought it was fine." You need the actual regulations.

As an entrepreneur operating in the mobile food service industry, it is your responsibility to know and understand the local regulations. Once you learn them, you should laminate them and keep them with you all the time.

Food Truck Regulations

Food truck regulations are going through lots of changes, and the information in this book could be out of date quickly. As the food truck trend grows, cities that have never regulated street food before are suddenly finding themselves generating new laws for food trucks.

Appendix B includes snapshots of the regulatory framework in several markets across the United States. This provides an overview to the rules and regulations that need to be followed by a food truck operator. Before opening a business, be sure to research and read up on the local rules of your municipality thoroughly, as regulations change frequently.

Typical Paradigms of Food Truck Regulation

Like the restaurant industry, food trucks are also heavily regulated. Regulations pertain to two key areas: truck construction and vending regulations. It is essential to thoroughly understand the regulatory rules in your municipality as they will impact every aspect of your business from start to finish.

Truck Types

One way in which food trucks are regulated pertains to the type of food that is served from a food truck. The common breakdown is between *processing trucks*, which serve food that has been prepared on the truck, like tacos, burgers, or waffles, and *nonprocessing trucks*, which serve prepackaged food that has been prepared off-site. The major distinguishing factor is that since processing trucks prepare foods with a risk for food-borne pathogens, they pose a greater risk to public health. With modern manufacturing processes, it is entirely possible to build trucks that can vend processed food safely. In time, local regulations will catch up with the reality.

Vending Locations

Some markets allow street vending on public streets. This is usually restricted in some way by hours or locations that are available. Usually trucks are required to vend a set distance away from other businesses selling similar products. While street vending can give you access to more vending locations, it is also challenging because there is often competition for the best locations.

Some municipalities allow food trucks or carts only in private lots. Lot vending has been very successful in markets like Portland and Austin. Lots have also been a very successful alternative even in markets where street vending is allowed, like New York City and Los Angeles.

Best Practices in Food Truck Regulation

Food trucks are great for cities. They get customers out on the street and create a sense of community. In addition to activating public space, food trucks offer local municipalities tax revenues and they stimulate job growth, tourism, and entrepreneurship. Most economists agree that small businesses are the major driver of job growth. Food trucks are hyper-local small businesses that develop the communities they vend in. They buy from local vendors, hire local employees, and sell to local customers. One of the most exciting aspects of food trucks is their ability to act as an incubator for entrepreneurs to start a viable, cash-flow positive business that can grow into a restaurant to become an even more stable part of the community from which they came. Food truck regulations are at their best when they promote public safety, avoid overcrowding of trucks, allow for competition, stimulate innovation, and are enforceable.

Food Trucks versus Restaurants

Food trucks and restaurants have a lot more in common than not. Senior vice president of the National Restaurant Association Hudson Riehle referred to food trucks as "mobile restaurant unit[s]."[17]

"Mobile restaurants" is an accurate representation of how most food trucks are operated. The word *restaurant* comes from the French verb *restaurer*, "to restore." Whether hospitality entrepreneurs operate as a restaurant, a deli, a kiosk, a cart, or a truck, all hospitality businesses are focused on the same core issues: to restore guests with great service and great food.

Competition is the nature of all business, including the hospitality business. There are restaurants, delis, grocery stores, and pharmacies all catering to the same customers. Food trucks and brick-and-mortar restaurants are two different business models that each have different strengths and weaknesses.

Interview 1: Matt Geller of SoCalMFVA on Food Truck Advocacy

Matt Geller is the founder and CEO of the Southern California Mobile Food Vendors' Association (SoCalMFVA). Matt is one of the foremost figures in food truck advocacy in the United States and has visited a number of cities across the country to promote mobile vending. For more information on SoCalMFVA please visit its website at: socalmfva.com.

Q: What trends have you noticed in mobile food legislation?

The biggest trend is acceptance. Cities around the country are starting to look at their regulations and make amendments. For years the industry was underground and very little attention was paid to operators and the rules that governed them. Now citizens are demanding access to food trucks, and cities must respond.

Q: What are the most common challenges food trucks face from a regulatory perspective across the country?

Arbitrary regulations are the biggest challenge. These are regulations that have no connection with any public safety concern or legitimate state (or city) interest. The regulations are usually created by established businesses that don't want to compete with the mobile food industry.

It's important for trucks to control the message. It's not an issue of unfair competition; it's an issue of consumer choice. We believe in competition in the United States, and it should be an important part of our message.

Q: Do you think that good rules lead to better food trucks for customers?

Limiting health permits or vending permits for food trucks has the most detrimental effect on the industry for customers. The market will work out winners and losers. If cities or counties cap the amount of permits issued, it allows the ones with permits to stop competing. It raises prices, lowers quality, and creates a black market for permits.

Good rules make good food trucks. Regulations should always have a public safety component. Arbitrary, anticompetitive rules restrict consumer choice and kill innovation.

Good Rules: Food safety, trash pickup, no smoking in truck, commissary cleanliness, distance from schools if applicable, water and restroom access.

Bad Rules: Permit caps, distance from brick-and-mortar businesses, time limitations (other than the posted signs), bans, bans from particular parts of town, and restrictions on private property use.

Q: What are the top three food truck cities from an operator's perspective? (In other words, where it is easy to operate?)

1. Los Angeles: There is an established industry in Los Angeles started by the traditional loncheros trucks. There are commissaries, truck builders and renters, and plenty of spaces to vend. The health department can be draconian, but SoCalMFVA has started to push back and get them to act responsibly. California doesn't allow regulations that are not in the interest of public safety, so bans and truck-specific regulations are nonexistent in most of the LA County cities. There is also no limit on the number of health permits that can be issued, so the market decides the winners and losers. Food truck lots and festivals are the norm now, and it makes vending a lot easier, because you know what to expect. Additionally, food trucks are now part of the mainstream. Health department inspection grades have helped overcome naysayers and change the old "roach coach" stereotypes.

Competition is an issue with over 230 gourmet trucks, but there are 88 cities and 66 unincorporated areas in Los Angeles County with a population of over 10 million. Eighty five of the cities and all of the unincorporated areas use LA County as their health department, so there are numerous places that trucks can go. Another issue is that all new trucks have to conform with very strict NSF standards.

2. Washington, DC: There are some serious restrictions on the size of a truck, 18.5 feet long, in Washington, DC. However, their building standards are not as crazy as those in Los Angeles, and their regulatory body falls under the District Consumer and Regulatory Affairs agency. While their regulations are still in flux, Sam Williams, who heads

(continued)

(continued)

the vending enforcement, is way ahead of the pack when it comes to providing a fair and equitable regulatory environment. The foodie scene coupled with the high-density population makes many places an attractive place to vend. The DC Food Truck Association is starting to do more events and find more lots to make the environment even better.

3. Denver (tied with Miami): Denver has lenient building standards and a population that loves the outdoors, even when it's cold. The city is still amending laws for mobile vending, but it is moving in the right direction. Additionally, many of the trucks on the road are connected to restaurants. This helps alleviate the complaints of unfair competition from restaurants.

4. Miami (tied with Denver): Regulations are light, and the industry is new. Residents of Miami and North Miami are loving the trucks. There is enough land to set up lots and festivals as well as amazing weather that allows a food truck to operate year-round. The truck building regulations are fair and appropriate for the industry.

The Importance of Advocacy

The nature of street vending has changed, and the rules that have been on the books since the turn of the century should change with it. As Matt has described, food trucks operators want to follow the rules: they just need fair and equitable laws to follow.

If there is an advocacy group in your city or town, consider joining to help them promote the industry. However, more than just paying dues, see what you can do to contribute to moving the advocacy effort forward.

If there isn't an advocacy group in your city, you might want to consider starting one. In markets that have a sizeable group of food trucks that are committed to innovation in hospitality, high-quality food, and community development, it is worthwhile working together to advocate for better laws. You'll need a core group of at least 15 to 20 vendors who are committed to the cause and who will contribute time and resources toward your shared goals.

Picking a Concept

Now THAT YOU have a good handle on the core regulatory requirements in your city or town, it is time to sit down and refine your concept. Before you even picked up this book, you probably had a good idea of what type of food truck you were hoping to run. In this chapter we're going to dig a bit deeper into your concept and think about the strengths and weaknesses of the concept and how to best roll it out on the streets.

Find a Great Story

Great businesses start like great stories: They are intriguing from the first sentence. They appeal to your dramatic sensibility. They include lots of details to make them real and relevant. They are internally consistent . . . and quite often they have a great ending!

For your business to be great, it needs to be compelling and make sense. All the core aspects of your concept need to be consistent. If you choose the right product and you sell it in the right place at the right time, you are going to be in great shape. If you chose a great product but try to sell it at the wrong place, your story won't make sense and your business won't work.

Here is a great story: Juan, who is Columbian-American, runs the Neira Coffee Cart. He imports coffee from a plantation near where his grandparents still live in Neira, Columbia. The Neira Coffee Cart serves coffee daily from 6:30 AM to 10:30 AM on a busy pedestrian sidewalk between a mass transit station and the city's largest office building.

This is a great story because every aspect is internally consistent. Juan has chosen the right product to serve the right customer at the right place at the right time. If you change any aspect of the story, it falls apart. It doesn't make any sense if Juan is out in his cart serving coffee at 8 PM.

31

Even if Juan has a lifelong passion for caramel corn and has developed the world's best recipe, serving it at 8 AM to commuters isn't going to work. Juan needs to move the caramel corn cart to a weekend street fair.

Key Criteria to Consider

Here are some things to consider as you develop and refine your concept. Ultimately you'll want to come up with a food truck concept that you are excited about, that will resonate with your customers, and that will ultimately be profitable.

Picking Your Passion

Operating a food truck is hard work. You need to love your product to succeed. Food is one of the most universal experiences, and cooking is a near universal skill. Sharing your passion for a particular cuisine or a particular dish that had a formative experience for you is essential.

Competitive Niche

My advice to most aspiring food truck entrepreneurs is to do one thing and do it well! Because the trucks have such limited space, it is important to be the best at whatever you are attempting to do. Except in very underdeveloped markets without much competition, trucks will rarely win at being a deli on wheels. Because trucks have such limited capacity, they will always lose to a restaurant that has more storage to provide a variety of options to guests.

Be the Best

People love good food. They like the best. You should strive to be the best at something that is accessible to the customers in your market. Fusion can be fun and exciting, but there are limits to how much change customers can tolerate. Usually customers are willing to try one new tweak on a classic. But two changes are often too much.

Food Fitness

It is important to understand that not all foods translate into successful food trucks. There are a number of constraints to a mobile kitchen that might prevent certain foods from being prepared safely, successfully, or profitably. Foods such as raw fish and others that require extremely safe handling are not well suited to trucks. Food that are extremely labor intensive or process oriented are not well suited to trucks. The best mobile food trucks often draw their inspiration from traditional street foods, like hot dogs, nuts, or ice cream, and give them a new twist.

Types of Food Trucks

The following list is of some of the food served from branded trucks in the United States. This is not meant to be an exhaustive list of all the possible or appropriate types of food trucks but simply a summary of the variety of options to help you brainstorm about your own niche.

Savory food trucks, in order of popularity

1. Burgers
2. Sandwiches
3. Barbecue
4. Hot dogs
5. Tacos
6. Mexican
7. Asian/Latin fusion
8. Pizza
9. Asian food
10. Organic
11. Greek/ Mediterranean
12. Grilled cheese
13. Cajun
14. Indian
15. Soup/chili
16. Seafood
17. Filipino
18. Schnitzel and sausages
19. Cuban
20. Italian
21. Latin, general
22. French fries
23. Southern food
24. Kebabs
25. Korean
26. Chinese
27. Breakfast
28. Thai
29. Lobster
30. French
31. Fusion
32. Health foods and salads
33. Hawaiian
34. Philly cheesesteaks
35. Falafel and pitas
36. Vegan/vegetarian
37. Meatballs
38. Tamales
39. Sushi
40. Japanese
41. Argentinean
42. Italian panini
43. Macaroni and cheese
44. Dumplings
45. Gyros
46. Caribbean
47. Sloppy joes
48. Wings
49. Spanish
50. Jamaican
51. Chicken and waffles
52. Fried chicken
53. Polish
54. Salvadorian
55. Czech
56. Bacon
57. Stews
58. Brazilian
59. Cheese

60. Fish and chips
61. Kosher
62. Malaysian
63. Pakistani
64. Peruvian
65. Pickles
66. Romanian
67. Sri Lankan
68. Swedish
69. Turkey
70. Venezuelan

Sweet trucks, in order of popularity

1. Ice pops/frozen treats
2. Cupcakes
3. Ice cream
4. General desserts
5. Bakery
6. Frozen yogurt
7. Chocolate
8. Doughnuts
9. Gelato
10. Churros
11. Crème brûlée
12. Nuts

Sweet/savory combination, in order of popularity

1. Crepes
2. Pies
3. Waffles
4. Empañadas
5. Popcorn
6. Peanut butter

Beverage trucks

1. Coffee/tea
2. Smoothies/juices

Licensing and Franchising

While the autonomy of owning a business is a primary part of the appeal of a food truck for most vendors, some first-time entrepreneurs might be interested in licensing or franchising a food truck. Food truck franchises are just getting started. There are a few concepts out there, but few are national in scope. Two notable franchises are Gandolfo's New York Delicatessen and Sâuçá (eatsauca.com). Franchises typically charge an up-front training fee in addition to the costs of the truck, plus a 4 to 6 percent franchise fee off gross revenues and an additional 1 to 2 percent marketing fee.

Licensing or franchising a food truck brand does have some advantages. First, you will be opting into a concept with an established brand, honed operations, and, presumably, a proven track record. You will get help and advice working out operational challenges that you might otherwise have to work out on your own. However, in return you will be giving up some of your profits in royalty fees. If you go the franchise route, one thing to be sure you work out is the extent of your territory. The fact that food trucks are mobile makes the concept of franchising territories much more complicated. Also, if the franchise sells both restaurant and food truck franchises, what are the boundaries of each? As a food truck owner, you won't want the franchise company to sell a restaurant franchise right on the corner of your best sales location.

One option to keep in mind is establishing a partnership with a restaurant that has a great product. You can offer to launch their mobile business for an equity stake in the new venture. Partnering with a restaurant will give you a head start as the menu, operations, and brand will already be established. You'll just need to translate them into something that works effectively on a truck.

It is worth noting that part of the appeal to food truck consumers is the idea that they are supporting an entrepreneur's dream. There is an intangible added value to meeting an owner operator on a truck and seeing your five dollars support their efforts to break free and succeed at their own project.

Competitive Analysis

Spend some time examining the market. Compare your concept with other concepts in your city, whether they are businesses or food trucks. Make a spreadsheet to summarize these businesses, their core menu offering, their price point, and the customers they appeal to. Figure out a specific niche for your concept that is unique to a customer base you can win.

Operations!

Consider a snapshot of your daily operations from start to finish. You don't need to solve every aspect of your operations yet, but you should have a good idea of what a day in the life of your food truck will look like. Where will you prep the food? Where will you store your truck? What time of day will you sell?

As you think about your concept, one major aspect to consider is the operational flow of your production. A major decision is to work out where your food is produced and how far that production is taken at whatever facilities are at your disposal. What products do you buy from vendors versus those you make in-house? What happens in the commissary? What is prepped on the truck at the start of the shift? What is prepared to order? All of these decisions will have a big impact on the infrastructure requirements of your business, the operational flows of your daily routine, and the revenue targets of your business. For instance, while you could bake cookies on your truck, it might be more efficient to pick up cookies from a commissary or a vendor each morning.

Where Is the Magic?

Food trucks are very transparent. Customers can look into the window and see the entire operation. As you think about where to cut the production chain, you need to consider the pros and cons of the value created by different components of production. For instance, you want to do the most special or value-added component of the process at the end. If it is at all possible, put it on display. If you sell crème brûlée, for example, the most dramatic element comes at the end of the production of the dessert, torching the top of the crème to create a caramelized crust. If you sell cupcakes, try to save space in your truck to have someone frosting them. If you sell pizza, let the customers see you toss them or lay out the toppings. The more you can add to the overall experience for your customers, the more value they'll get out of the purchase . . . and the more likely that they'll be back again, not just for the food, but for the show.

Interview 2: Kim Ima of The Treats Truck on Developing a Brand

Kim Ima is one of the pioneers of the new wave of branded food trucks in New York City. Kim opened The Treats Truck (TheTreatsTruck.com) in 2007 to serve simple but delicious treats. Kim's delicious treats have won her a loyal following of fans and also recognition in the form of a Vendy Award for Best Dessert Vendor. The success of The Treats Truck has lead to a book published in 2011, *The Treats Truck Baking Book: Cookies, Brownies & Goodies Galore!* Kim is currently working on opening a bakery and café in Carroll Gardens, Brooklyn, The Treats Truck Stop (TheTreatsTruckStop.com).

Q: When you started your truck, was it based on an existing brand, or was it a totally new concept?

Totally new!

Q: If you invented your brand, can you talk a little about the process? Who did you brainstorm with? How did you choose a single idea?

I love branding. I was guided by my experience with brands as a customer. I have an awesome graphic designer, and we worked for about eight months on branding and other preparations before I opened the truck. I kept inspiration books full of examples of brands and logos that I liked. We spent about two and a half months developing the logo. It's 1950s inspired but at the same time fresh and modern. We chose colors that were timeless (not likely to go out of style). I developed a voice to use on the website and on the truck. ("This truck runs on compressed natural gas and chocolate.") I tested recipes and worked on naming the treats. I gave out free cookies at entrepreneurs' events to test out the concept. Food trucks are kind of like carousel horses: customers choose them based on the look. The branding process was really fun. The brand is part of what I giving to my customers.

Q: How do you promote your brand?

The truck itself, T-shirts, recipe book, business cards, website, Twitter, Facebook, and magazine articles.

Q: How did you establish the quality of your brand?

The product has to be good. The customer relations and the experience have to be special—for example, when someone orders a brownie, we always ask, "Do you want a middle, edge, or corner piece?" The website has to look very professional. And consistency in our parking schedule is helpful, because then we get regulars and create a kind of rapport with each neighborhood.

(continued)

(continued)

Q: Did you advertise your brand before your truck opened, or did you let it hit the streets as a wild card?

We publicized it about a month before—just long enough to create some buzz, but not long enough for people to forget or get tired of it. We did a "coming soon" magazine story.

Q: Have you considered expanding your business and having more than one establishment under the same brand?

I had two trucks for a while, but I went back to one truck in less than a year because two was too much to organize by myself. I could see maybe having a sister truck in a different city with its own manager but never a franchise. I don't want to leave New York. At first I was thinking of opening in Los Angeles because I have family there, but "my heart was in my shoes" because I love New York too much. I am opening a café/bakery in Carroll Gardens called The Treats Truck Stop, and that's exciting. I'm going to split my time between the truck and the bakery. Right now I drive the truck every day, about six days a week (seven during the holidays). Mondays are my day off, except when it's super cold, and then I take Sundays off.

Q: That sounds exhausting. How do you handle it?

Interacting with the customers makes it all worth it. It reminds me why I do this.

Q: Do you have any promotional ideas to share with aspiring food truck entrepreneurs?

Punch cards work great. Also, I give out a free cookie when customers bring in my recipe book, The Treats Truck Baking Book, to get it signed. And, of course free stickers for kids. Kids love stickers!

The Right Format

There are a number of ways to execute your concept. One of the primary factors that will dictate the best type of mobile food unit will be the local municipal regulations. Some markets, like Portland, are mostly carts; some markets, like Austin, are mostly trailers; and some markets, like Los Angeles, are mostly trucks. Mobile food units have much more in common than not. However, each application has different pros and cons, so it is worth considering if your concept might be even more effective as a trailer, a cart, a kiosk, or a restaurant.

Trucks

Food trucks offer a high degree of flexibility and ease of use. Because the kitchen of the food truck is on the bed of the truck, it makes it simple to transport and park. The downside of food trucks is that if the truck breaks down, you cannot get your kitchen where you need to go. Because of their size, food trucks are highly visible. Aside from being a viable business in their own right, they will help promote your brand and keep your business at the top of your customers' minds. Depending on the type of food you are planning to sell, a truck could be perfect. Ice cream novelties and soft-serve ice cream have been sold from trucks for decades because the food product is fast to serve and the mobility of the unit lets them serve many customers while out serving a route. Many gourmet food trucks use their trucks primarily as a destination and might move only once or twice a day to serve different meal periods in different locations. Food trucks come in a variety of shapes and sizes. Small trucks are great in urban areas where parking is limited, as they can better fit into a parking spot when a car leaves. However, smaller trucks mean less capacity. Big trucks are great for special events. One day in the fall of 2011, Dunkin' Donuts provided coffee off a truck with a 24-foot bed that would be impossible to park in Manhattan but that was perfect for serving 500 gallons of coffee to the tens of thousands of runners who were waiting in the cold to start the New York City Marathon.

Trailers

Food trailers are usually built out pretty similarly to the bed of a food truck. The major distinction between a food truck and a trailer is that trailers aren't self-propelled. Buying your trailer and truck separately is usually a bit less expensive than building out a food truck. It also gives you more flexibility to repair and maintain your equipment. If the truck you use to pull your trailer gets a flat, your business won't be down for the day; instead, you can rent a truck from Ryder and still work the lunch shift. However, when a food truck gets a flat, the business isn't making money until the repair is made. The downside to trailers is that moving them is a bit more involved. Because of their large size, they will require a strong truck and some effort. Many entrepreneurs get the most out of their trailers by parking them by the week or the month at a stable location. If you plan on keeping your business relatively stationary, a trailer might be a good idea. One challenge for trailers is the wastewater or gray water they generate. Different municipalities have different rules about wastewater, but water from food operations should never be dumped on the ground of a lot or poured down a sewer. Often local portable toilet vendors will be able to collect and correctly process gray water.

Carts

The biggest pros and cons of food carts are related to their size. Because of their smaller footprint and the fact that they aren't a vehicle, carts have an advantage in being placed in locations where trucks or trailers might not be able to go, like on a sidewalk or deep in a pedestrian mall. However, since they are smaller, carts have less visibility and less capacity. Carts have a limited street presence. Carts are best suited to concepts with very limited menus like coffee, hot dogs, pretzels, cupcakes, nuts, popsicles, or ice cream. In urban areas, if you have a central depot or commissary, carts can be walked or propelled with small motors to get them placed. However, most carts require a truck or van to place them daily and often require the storage of a van to get through multiple service periods. Moving a cart daily is challenging physical labor, and it will take practice to back it up properly.

Kiosks

Kiosks are temporary, moveable, but not mobile structures that are often erected in high foot-traffic areas to support demand for food on the go. Kiosks are generally less expensive than building out a restaurant because they are semipermanent. Also, they are smaller and usually feature only a kitchen/service area without a seating area. Kiosks can be assembled indoors in large spaces like convention centers or transit hubs, or outdoors in parks or pedestrian plazas. Like semipermanent trailers, dealing with wastewater can sometimes be a challenge if your kiosk isn't attached to a sewer main.

Restaurants

Before you jump into the realm of mobile food, be sure you have done your due diligence on looking at restaurant spaces as well. Restaurants offer a lot of advantages that you will miss on the streets, and depending on your business model, it might make sense to start with a single restaurant and then grow the brand with a truck or two. Restaurants tend to have high front-end capital costs for the deposit and build-out of the property. Restaurants also tend to have slightly higher fixed costs as they are paying rent monthly. However, if you negotiated your rent well and found a good location, you should get a fair value for those expenses. Restaurants are safe and stable. With few exceptions, restaurants tend to have much higher revenues than mobile food units. They provide a controlled environment for your guests to enjoy their meal. If you are in a city that is very cold (or very hot) a restaurant might be a more sound business decision. Restaurants can also apply for a license to sell alcohol, which is a very high margin item that can never be sold on the streets.

Customers

Think about who will be eating your food. The most important stakeholder in your business will be your customers, so it is important to create a valuable offering that appeals to them. Certain decisions you make might disenfranchise you with certain demographics but can win you dedicated followers in others. It is important to be consistent with your product, branding, and operations so that you offer the right product to the right people at the right time.

- **Office workers:** Office workers and busy professionals are often looking for tasty food, fast. The key purchasing times for this demographic are the morning commute, lunch hour, and sometimes afternoon snack time. Office workers tend to hurry home for dinner.

- **Tourists:** Tourists are in the city to shop, run errands, or see the sights. Tourists can be found around parks, museums, art galleries, and important landmarks during the day. They are usually looking for safe, clean food that is convenient.
- **Late-night revelers:** In cities with good weather and a lot of night-life, vendors can do a thriving business late into the evening and early into the morning. Indulgent, greasy foods tend to sell better to late-night revelers.
- **Parents with kids:** Depending on where you are vending, you may want to have a kid-friendly menu with smaller portions and more accessible menu items. If you are vending near a park, a playground, or a mall, winning over the kids will be very important. Children are very influential in getting their parents to eat where they want. Help your cause by offering healthy, but tasty, options for kids.

Vending Locations

There are a number of places you can sell. You don't need to negoti-ate a contract or pick a spot before you write your business plan, but you should have a good idea of where you plan to vend because dif-ferent people go to different places, and it influences the types of food that are most relevant and the pricing that is acceptable. Common vending locations include the street and, if legal in your municipality, malls, parks, central business districts, college campuses, office parks, manufacturing plants, and food truck lots.

Naming Your Truck

Naming your business is an extremely important part of capturing the essence of your business. Ultimately, your business will be judged by the quality of its goods and products. Think of a name as the frame-work on which your customers hang their understanding of the value of your brand.

What's in a Name?

All things being equal, neutral names are preferable because you can layer your own meaning on them. However, giving some flavor to the concept through the name can help define the business, especially at the start when you are looking for new customers.

If you end up choosing a descriptive name, be sure that the name is consistent with the brand identity you want to convey. "Flash Burger" sounds fast. "Local Burger" implies you are sourcing local ingredients. On the flip side, the name should be relevant but not constraining. You should think about the long-term growth potential of your plans. If you call your business "Bob's Burger Truck" and after a year or two you want to settle down and open a restaurant, "truck" isn't so ideal. Or if you end up discovering that two-thirds of your sales are hot dogs you might want to drop the "burger" from the name.

The name should be accessible to your target customer. Foreign words should be kept to a minimum unless they are readily understood and easy to pronounce. Most of the population is familiar with Spanish, French, and Italian culinary words. Be sure to test out more exotic names on a sample group. While your friends can give you advice, they probably are of similar backgrounds and dispositions and may come to the same conclusions that you do. You should try to get your customers' perspectives as much as possible. Don't be afraid to ask them yourself. Go to a corner where you would potentially be vending and poll pedestrians about which truck they'd most likely eat from: Bob's Burgers, Flash Burger, or Local Burger.

Finally, think about different variations of the name, such as double entendres and obvious puns. If you call your business "Flash Burger" but it takes you 15 minutes to get out a burger, you can be sure critics and bloggers will be taking note.

Checking for the Rights

As part of your research on naming your business, you should check if the name is currently already in use. Because online marketing is so important, you should take pains to find a name for which you can secure the domain name, Facebook name, and Twitter handle. It is ideal to get the same name for all three so that it is easy for your customers to find you online. The most restrictive naming convention is Twitter, with its 15-character limit, so that is the best place to start finding a name.

You should also check for trademarks on file already using the name. Especially if you are hoping to grow outside your home state, you'll want to search the US Patent and Trademark Office by going to this URL: uspto.gov/trademarks/index.jsp.

If you have the time, you can file for the trademark on your own, but unless you know what you're doing, it is probably worth hiring someone to help you legally secure the rights for your brand.

Key Metrics

Before building out an entire business plan around your food truck, it is important to test a few economic fundamentals to make sure that your food truck will be profitable.

The economic foundations of a viable food truck are based on five basic principles:

1. Throughput
2. Average sales per guest
3. Cost of goods sold
4. Capacity
5. Breakeven

Throughput

Throughput is the measure of speed. It is how fast on average you can prepare meals for your guests. Usually it is quoted as the number of guests per hour. It is good to test this as an average over time to discern what the bottleneck in your operations might be. Usually the bottleneck is associated with a piece of equipment, for example, a panini press that can hold only four sandwiches at a time or a grill that can cook only 12 burgers. To get at your throughput, you should test how fast you can assemble one item. This is the theoretical maximum. Then you need to test how fast you can keep up that speed over time. Your throughput is one constraint on the revenue capacity of your truck. Whenever possible, you should test out the equipment you will be using to see what you can realistically do. However, if you don't have real equipment, you can model it and then role-play.

Sweet trucks typically have few problems with throughput. If you are carrying premade cupcakes, you can sell as fast as people can hand you money. However, if you are making burgers to order, your operations are going to be limited by the grill. Savory trucks should look to be able to do throughputs of 100 guests per hour. Sweet trucks should be able to do double that.

In general, faster is better. The faster your truck is, the more customers you can serve and the more money you can make. The faster your truck is, the less likely it is that you might get a "walk away"—a customer who is interested in your food enough to queue but doesn't have the patience to wait for the time they think it will take to get an order.

Try some real life tests with the equipment you are planning to use. Because trucks have limited power supply if your cooking equipment is electric, it may not be as powerful as a version in a restaurant. You also need to incorporate the heat loss if you are operating at max throughput. If you are using a panini press, every time you put a new sandwich on the grill, it cools it down. You may grill a sandwich in five minutes, but if you are doing sandwich after sandwich it may slow down to seven minutes per press. The same goes for a steamer or a pizza oven. Every time you open the equipment, the heat will escape and slow down cook times.

Average Sales per Guest

Average sales per guest is a measure of the average transaction size on a truck. Let's say there is a hypothetical burger truck with a menu of burgers for $6, fries for $2, and drinks for $1 and that the typical customer gets a burger, half of customers get fries, and half also get a drink. The average sales per guest would be $7.50. The average sales per guest times the throughput gives you a theoretical maximum to the revenue capacity for the truck. If this burger truck could serve 100 customers per hour, they could make $750 per hour, maximum.

Your average sales are dictated by the menu mix and the prices that you can command for the items on your menu. In general, as an entrepreneur you will want to maximize the amount of revenue you can earn per guest, while still having guests feel like they got a good value.

Pricing is a very complicated process that is half art and half science. There is a chapter devoted to food cost and pricing later in the book. To get started, you should set prices at levels that are comparable to other restaurants or food trucks that sell similar products. Try to improve the value to your customers by lowering the price or buying better ingredients if you can afford it.

Your average sales per guest times the number of sales you can make per day will give you a good idea of your revenue.

Cost of Goods Sold

Costs of goods sold (COGS) is a common accounting term that captures the variable cost of each sale. All the variable costs associated with an order should be captured in this number. Typically COGS includes food costs, paper costs, and labor costs associated with food production (not the labor to serve the food). In the restaurant industry, a typical target COGS is around 30 percent. If you can run at numbers lower than that, it is great. However, always keep an eye toward value. If you run at 15 percent COGS, you might be making more money, but customers may not sense the value. If you lose customers, you may have a hard time earning them back.

To test the viability of your food truck business, you should figure out the food cost of the primary item you will be selling. If you are a burger truck, this is a burger; if you are a waffle truck, this is a waffle. You need to be sure that you can buy the ingredients you need and sell at a price people will buy.

For example, if you are going to sell a burger with regular ground beef priced at $2.60 per pound, you may find your food costs are as follows:

4 oz. ground beef	$0.65
Bun	0.35
Veggies	0.10
Condiments	0.05
Wrapper	0.05
Total:	$1.20

If you price your burgers at $4.00, you'd be in good shape as your theoretical COGS would be at around 30 percent. However, if you were trying to sell all-natural, locally sourced beef burgers at $4 each, you might get into trouble. If all-natural, grass-fed local beef is $5.45

per pound, then the COGS for this item would shoot up to $1.91, which would make the COGS about 48 percent. To price that item in the zone of profitability, you'd want to price it at $6.25 or $6.50.

Actual COGS will always be worse than your theoretical COGS. Some extra burgers might get made that aren't sold, and these are waste. Once your burgers are cooked, you cannot recover them to sell later. Another possibility is shrinkage, which is when employees help themselves to extra meals on the side or give out food to friends or regulars without accounting for it.

You should include the labor it takes to prepare menu items in the COGS. If you have an amazing soup that takes you 10 hours of chopping and simmering, even if the food cost looks like it is 15 percent or 20 percent, it might actually be at 40 percent if you include the labor.

Capacity

Capacity refers to the amount of food storage available on your truck. In particular, how many guests can you serve? For example, on our burger truck we have perhaps enough storage on board to sell to 500 customers. This also lets us know that if our average check is $7.50, the highest revenue we could expect to make per day is $3,750. Also, if we are selling at our maximum throughput, we would be sold out in five hours.

Breakeven

The breakeven is an important "back of the envelope" calculation to determine the tipping point between losing money and starting to make money on a shift. To calculate the breakeven, you solve for revenue by using the following equation:

$$\text{Revenue} \times \text{COGS} - \text{Labor} - \text{Costs/Shift} - \text{Fixed Costs} = \text{Profit}$$

For the breakeven, we know profit is 0, so we can rewrite the equation as follows:

$$\text{Revenue (Breakeven)} = (\text{Labor} + \text{Costs/Shift} + \text{Fixed Costs})/1\text{-COGS}$$

Again for our burger truck, let's say a typical shift has service from 11 AM to 3 PM with two hours of setup and breakdown on either side. That is an eight-hour day for two staff people, or 16 hours of work time. If these truck employees are making $11 per hour, the labor cost is $176.

Costs per shift might be fuel fees, tolls, parking fees, or location fees in order to vend at a lot for the day. For our burger example, let's say these are $25 per day.

Fixed costs are the larger expenses of the business, such as commissary rent, insurance, bookkeeper fees, lawyer fees, website fees, and so forth. For our burger example, let's say these are $100 per day.

$$\text{Revenue (Breakeven)} = (176 + 25 + 100)/(1 - .30) = \$430$$

This is 58 customers, or, in our 11 AM to 3 PM window, 14.5 customers per hour.

This number is the sales you'll need to do each day to breakeven. To make money, you'll need to make a bit more to outrun the depreciation on your initial investments.

Sweet trucks, because they generally sell prepared items for lower prices, like cookies or ice cream, usually have faster throughputs and lower average checks.

Putting It All Together

Before you dig into a business plan, you should be able to summarize quickly what your food truck is all about. Take a moment to write out a few sentences to explain your food truck, your core menu items, your target customers, potential vending locations, the basics of the operations, and your commissary location. If everything seems consistent, you're in good shape. This is the core of the executive summary for your business plan.

Assembling a Winning Team

THE MOST IMPORTANT aspect for any business is the people. As the founder of your food truck business, you will be extremely instrumental in getting your business to market, but no one can make it on their own. Depending on your background and your resources, you may be thinking of having a partner. You will definitely be looking for assistance from a number of professionals who may include a fabricator, mechanic, lawyer, or accountant.

Experienced venture capital investors that invest in early stage start-ups tend to list the core team as the most important criteria in assessing the prospects of a new business investment. This is because the experience, skills, and resourcefulness of the founding team make a significant difference in if a business will get started, if it can be run profitably, and if it will survive.

Hospitality Is about Execution

There is no intellectual property in hospitality. Anyone can copy anyone else's business model or recipes. The major differentiators are food types, branding, and execution. At the end of the day, you will be judged on how well you can operate consistently at a very high level of excellence. Operating well consistently is very hard, and the only way it gets done is with the oversight of excellent, engaged operators.

Business Partners

A great business partner can be really, really great. And a bad business partner can be really, really bad. You should be extremely thoughtful as you think about bringing on a partner in your business. The key is

49

to find a partner who has a very similar vision of where the business should go but very different professional strengths. If both partners are chefs, there is bound to be trouble over creative control in the kitchen, but if one partner went to culinary school and another studied accounting, the chances of long-term success are much better. You want to complement each other. Each partner should bring tangible value to the business. Some partners bring expertise, some bring relationships, and some bring money. And some bring the sweat, determination, and drive to get the business on the road.

One key thing to keep in mind is that the more partners who are involved in a venture, the less equity there is to go around. If you go for it on your own, you'll own 100 percent of the company. If you add one partner (on equal terms) you'll be at 50 percent. With two partners, you're already at 33 percent.

Key Hires

An alternative to bringing on a business partner is to bring on a key hire. But you could bring on an experienced food service professional as an operating manager for a truck with a good salary and some equity in the business. For a small business like a food truck, it won't make sense for you to hire your own accountant.

Professional Services

You should start looking now for professional assistance in the following areas: accounting, bookkeeping, graphic design, law, truck repairs, generator repairs, and web design. Unless you used to work as a professional in one of these vocations (and want to do it for your own business), you should have a professional resource in your list of contacts to call for help when you need it. A responsive and responsible vendor who cares about you and your business can make a profound difference in the long-term viability of your business.

You probably have a few professional service vendors you know and trust already. Do not simply do a Google search for a lawyer or an accountant and hire the first one you find. Take the time to meet these folks and gauge how interested they are in you and your business.

The Business Plan

A BUSINESS PLAN is a necessity to raise capital for your business from anyone besides your parents. However, even if you are going to invest only your own money into this business, you should really take the time to write out a business plan to help you anticipate challenges and keep you focused (and on budget) once you start your food truck.

There are a number of great books out there that can help you write great business plans. For more help with the specifics of writing a business plan, you can take a look at *The Ernst & Young Business Plan Guide* by Brian Ford, Jay Bornstein, and Patrick Pruitt or *Business Model Generation* by Alexander Osterwalder and Yves Pigneur. There are lots of great resources on this topic. This chapter is going to focus on some specific food truck issues as they relate to your business plan.

Key Assumptions

Before you dig into your business plan, you will need to know:

- The amount of time you will be devoting to this project (full time or part time)
- The minimum amount of money you need to make from the business to survive
- The core menu offering
- The scope of operations
- The weekly operating schedule (what shifts and what days of the week)

Overview of Key Accounting Terms

I am including a few key accounting terms that I will be using in the next chapter. If you are familiar with these terms, you can skip this section. If you don't have a solid understanding of these terms it might be worth taking some time to get a quick primer from your accountant or even spending some time to take an introductory accounting class. You don't need to know how to do bookkeeping or accounting, but being able to quickly interpret the data will help you in two important ways: it will help you run your business better, and it will help you to communicate with investors or loan officers when you are looking for funding.

■ **Balance sheet:** The balance sheet measures the current financial stock of your business. It provides a snapshot of the assets, liabilities, and capital for a specific point in time. Following are a list of the key items that will appear on the balance sheet of a food truck business:

o *Assets*: Assets are items of value that your business owns. They are usually listed in order of decreasing liquidity. Assets include the cash in your bank account; receivables you're waiting to collect on, such as unpaid credit card fees; and inventory, such as food you've purchased that hasn't yet been sold.

o *Liabilities*: Liabilities are the obligations of your business. They are usually listed in order of decreasing due date. The first thing might be accounts payable, or the amount for anything you bought from vendors on credit; next might be an account called sales tax payable to track the sales tax you owe; and, finally, if you took on any loans, they would appear in this section.

o *Capital*: Capital is the ownership stake of different investors in the business. If you are a sole proprietor, your capital would initially be the value that you invested in the business. Over time, if you are making money, you will accumulate retained earnings!

■ **Cash flow statement:** The cash flow statement measures changes in account balances over time. For instance, if the cash in your account went from $100,000 to $50,000, this would mean that you lost money in your operations. But it would be understandable if you used the $50,000 to invest in a truck to start your business. A cash flow statement is structured in the following categories:

o *Operating*: This is the net cash of sales minus expenses. It is extremely important to always keep this number positive. Small businesses need to generate cash to survive!

o *Investing*: Investing is usually cash outflows, such as purchases of assets (like your new truck).

o *Financing*: Financing is usually cash inflows from investors or bank loans.

- **Income statement:** The income statement, which is sometimes referred to as the profit and loss statement, measures the performance of the company. The income statement shows what revenues were earned and the costs and expenses it took to earn those revenues. Hospitality professionals often lay out their profit and loss statements in the following manner:

o Revenue

o Cost of goods sold (COGS)

o Gross profit

o Labor costs

o Operating costs

o Occupancy costs

o Management costs

o Net income

- **Variable costs:** These are costs that are directly related to sales. The best example of variable costs is the cost for the food or paper products.
- **Fixed costs:** These are costs that don't depend on sales. Examples of fixed costs are things like commissary rent, phone bills, or manager salaries.
- **Sunk costs:** Sunk costs are costs that have already been paid that cannot be recovered. Economically, these aren't relevant to evaluating future business decisions.

The Outline of a Business Plan

This is a brief outline of the standard components of a business plan:

- **Executive summary:** A pithy overview of the core business offering and key economics. This should be no longer than one page. You can use the executive summary as a teaser when you meet potential investors.

- **Products and services:** A description of the truck's menu and operations. Provide as much detail as you can about menu items and proof that you have done your research about food costs.
- **Industry analysis:** A description of the mobile food industry but specific to your municipality. Be sure to highlight all the relevant legal regulations that dictate your operations.
- **Competitive analysis:** Who else is out there? Look at your competition from other mobile food vendors, geographically in the neighborhoods you plan to vend for both trucks and stores, and finally by food type. For instance, if you are going to do a BBQ truck, how will you make your truck relevant in the mobile food scene in the city (pick a new color for your truck to stand out?), how are you different in the neighborhoods where you vend (no other BBQ available?), and how do you stand against all the other BBQ joints in the city (do you offer special rub or special sauce?)?
- **Marketing and sales:** A description of your marketing plans. Also, a major driver of food trucks is social media. Be sure to incorporate a social media plan, including Facebook and Twitter.
- **Management:** An overview of your team. Investors tend to look favorably on ventures where principals have experience in the industry and a history of starting successful companies. Potential investors will judge the management team on their ability to execute the business plan.
- **Operations:** A description of how the business will operate: Where will you vend? Where will you produce the food? How is the truck laid out? How fast can you serve customers? You should work out the operations well enough so that all you need is to add money and you can start your business.
- **Financial plan:** A rigorous overview of the financial costs to open the business and the expected financial performance once it is operating. If you live somewhere with seasons, be sure to include a one-year plan broken out by months that represent both the busy and slow seasons.
- **Financial requirements:** A summary of the money you need to get started.

In general, the softer part of the business plan should go pretty quickly. You've probably been thinking about your food truck business for a while, so you'll have a good idea of the concept, the food you plan on serving, and how it fits into the culinary landscape of your city. Most of the entrepreneurs I meet with are most concerned with coming up with a realistic pro forma financial plan.

Opening Costs

The primary cost for opening your business will be the expense of the food truck itself. You will also have expenses associated with the initial purchase of food and paper products and labor expenses for any training period prior to opening. According to the PBS, the average cost of opening a food truck is only $30,000 to $80,000.[21] This range seems a bit low to me, but the amount of money you can spend opening a food truck depends a lot on whether you are renting or buying and the type of truck you procure.

It is possible to rent a food truck with a $5,000 deposit, which would still give you $25,000 to wrap the truck, buy smallwares and the opening inventory, train staff, set up a website, and pay a deposit at a commissary. Alternatively, you could spend $100,000 on a new step van, another $50,000 building out the kitchen, and another $50,000 getting your business started, for a total of $200,000.

In general, you'll probably need at least $50,000 to start a food truck business with a rental food truck, $100,000 to start a food truck business in a used food truck, and $200,000 to start a food truck business in a new food truck. However, these costs could vary for a lot of reasons. The important thing about opening costs is to not miss anything. If you aren't careful, you could end up short on cash before you even get started—for example, if you forget to budget for buying your initial food inventory. Make a line item for everything you can think of in your budget, and then add a 10 percent miscellaneous fee to have a bit of a buffer for any unexpected costs that come along.

Modeling Revenue

Calculating the theoretical revenue of your food truck business will be one of the most challenging aspects of developing your business plan. A food truck could generate revenue from next to nothing to over $1 million depending on the type of food, the operation, and the location of the business. Based on a study of food trucks' credit card activity, it has been estimated that gourmet food trucks make $65,000 per month in cash and credit sales at the high end, with $20,000 being the midline.[21] This would suggest that an average food truck makes $240,000 per year in revenue and a high-end truck makes $780,000 a year in revenue. Food trucks with a high average "sales per guest," food trucks that can sell fast, and food trucks in densely populated areas will tend to have higher revenues.

There are a number of ways to try to back out the theoretical sales of your truck by looking at comparable businesses (comps), calculating from the top down, or by calculating from the bottom up. It is important to keep in mind that these will all be approximations for the sales your truck can do. The goal is to come up with the best estimate you can.

Comps

First, you should look at how the other hospitality businesses are performing in locations that are similar to where you plan to vend. You should research other trucks in your city as well as other brick-and-mortar restaurants. Go out and see these businesses in person. Talk to the owners if you can. Some business owners are very forthcoming about their sales; others are more discrete.

You should also make a point of watching the traffic flow of customers at businesses near where you plan to vend or businesses that sell a similar product. Before you head out on a research mission, buy a "hand tally counter" online or at an office supply store to keep in your pocket and then hit the streets to see how many customers your competition is getting. By watching their customers, you'll learn more about how to make your own business relevant and also get a good approximation of the sales done per day. The best way is to count the number of customers they have for a busy period and then extrapolate their sales per day, per week, and per year.

Top-Down Calculations

Publically traded companies publish unit economics that can be perused on financial websites like finance.yahoo.com. In annual reports, you can often see average sales per unit, sometimes even broken down by geography for companies like Chipotle, Burger King, or Così. Many franchises publish sales per unit online in the hope of attracting franchisees.

A good way to estimate what your revenues might be is to look for comps in similar restaurant businesses. If you plan to sell deli sandwiches, try to find out how the local Subway sandwich shops are performing. If you plan to sell pizza, try to find out how a local pizzeria is performing. A food truck will typically do about 20 to 40 percent of the sales of a similarly placed brick-and-mortar business.

Be sure to discount your potential sales further if you are comparing your business against a strong brand. For example, if you are opening a new burger truck, you will not have the marketing power of McDonald's!

Bottom-Up Calculations

The most accurate way to estimate your sales might be to calculate what your sales might be from the bottom up. You can do this by multiplying your average sales per guest by the number of guests you expect to serve per day.

To be as accurate as possible, calculate the number of guests you plan to see on a weekly basis. It might be easier to break it down by meal period as well. If you collected competitive research on the numbers of customers that different business served during a lunch rush, this will help you calculate the sales per hour.

Assuming average sales per guest = $7.50:

Mon.	Tues.	Wed.	Thurs.	Fri.	Sat.	Sun.	Total
Off	100	100	150	200	200	100	850

850 covers × $7.50 = $6,375 per week

If you are in Miami, maybe you can do this 50 weeks a year for a total of $318,750.

Use Three Scenarios

Based on your research, you should come up with a best-case and a worst-case scenario for how your business might plausibly perform. Using those two extremes, come up with a scenario you think is realistic. Try to make your realistic scenario as conservative as you can manage and still hit a reasonable profit. Once you write the business plan, it will become the yardstick by which your actual operation is measured. You might be tempted to plug in high revenues to make the numbers look good in the plan to make it easier to raise the funds you need. However, once you get the money in, you'll need to hit the numbers you have committed yourself to. In general, it is a good policy to *underpromise* and *overdeliver*. Behavioral economics teaches us that losses feel much worse than gains, so it is a good strategy to preemptively give yourself a bit of wiggle room to hit the goals you are setting for yourself.

Seasonality

Seasonality is an important element to incorporate into both of your business plans. Seasonality impacts the revenue expectations and also the cash demands on your business. If you are in a very seasonal market like Boston, New York, Seattle, or Portland, it is important to discount your sales in the winter months when there will be fewer customers out on the street. Also, for certain businesses, like ice cream or frozen treat sellers, it probably won't even be worth operating in the winter. Accurately modeling for the winter storage costs and also the costs (and effort) associated with reopening the business each spring must be considered. Ask around to see how street vendors fare in the slow season in your municipality. If you have no other information, discount sales by at least 30 percent.

If we go back to the bottom-up calculation but assume we are in Boston instead of Miami, we might come up with a very different estimate.

Assuming average sales per guest = $7.50:

Mon.	Tues.	Wed.	Thurs.	Fri.	Sat.	Sun.	Total
Off	100	100	150	200	200	100	850

850 covers × $7.50 = $6,375 per week

If we are in Boston, maybe you can do this 25 weeks a year and expect that during another 25 weeks your sales will be down 30 percent due to cold weather.

$$=\$6,375 \times 25 + \$6,375 \times 25 \times (1 - .3) = \$270,937$$

Considering Costs

Some approximate numbers to work with based on looking at the profit and loss statement might be:

Revenue

Cost of goods sold (COGS)   34%

Gross profit

Labor costs	26%
Operating costs	20%
Occupancy costs	8%
Management costs	7%
Net income	5%

COGS

The industry average for COGS is around 30 percent. This will vary depending on the type of product you are selling. If you sell popsicles (sugar and water) your COGS may run lower. If you sell lobster rolls, because your raw food costs are very expensive, your COGS could be in excess of 50 percent. You could estimate this price by looking at publically listed comps, but you might be better served by calculating this number from the bottom up off the theoretical food costs for your menu items and then adding a 5 percent premium for waste.

Labor

This is the cost for your employees' wages. The industry average for labor is around 30 percent. Your labor will depend on the amount of expertise you need from your employees. If you know the days and shifts your truck will be in operation, it is relatively simple to calculate this number theoretically from the bottom up. First determine the number of employees you need per shift and the number of shifts you need. Then multiply by the prevailing wage. Don't forget to add payroll taxes (which might be 10-12 percent). Then divide labor by sales for the same period.

Shifts per day: 2

Hours per shift: 6

Employees per shift: 1

Wages: $10 per hour

Payroll tax: 12%

Labor costs per day = 12 hours per day
× $10 hours × (1.12)

Labor costs per day = $134.40

If expected sales per day = $500

Labor % = Labor/Sales = 26.9%

Reality Check: Generally speaking, it is unlikely (but not impossible) that you will be able to come up with a food service business where the COGS and labor together are less than 50 percent. Lowering food costs usually requires either more preparation time or more service to command a premium price from customers. Although customers won't know your cost structure, they will have a sense of value based on other options in the market. If your "bottom-up" math yields numbers less than 50 percent, you should review your assumptions carefully.

Operating Costs

Operating costs is the catchall for general operating expenses. Gasoline, propane, office supplies, cleaning supplies, miscellaneous tools, linens, liability insurance, and merchant services all go into operating costs. This also includes professional services such as lawyers, bookkeepers, accountants, or graphic designers.

Occupancy

For restaurants, occupancy costs are typically somewhere around 8 to 10 percent. In urban areas, occupancy costs are often higher, running 10 to 15 percent. Because food trucks pay lower rents as they park at commissaries and depots outside of central business districts, typically their occupancy costs for rent are a bit lower. However, costs like event fees, fuel costs, and parking tickets will push all this back toward a number that is probably in the zone of 7 to 10 percent of sales.

Estimate your occupancy costs by researching the local costs for depot parking and the use of a commissary or commercial kitchen space if you need one. Don't forget to set aside a budget for special events or vending fees if there are special events where you plan to sell.

Management Costs

Management costs are the oversight costs to coordinate your business. This might be where your salary would be incorporated. If you have a food truck that you think can earn $300,000, you'll be looking at a salary of $21,000. However, what usually happens for small business food trucks is that the owner is both working the truck and managing the truck. So part of your salary will come from managing the truck, and part of it will come from working shifts.

Net Income

You should strive to come up with a budget that generates a net income of at least a 10 percent profit. If you are coming up with a net income in excess of 25 percent, you might be missing something. You will need to review the numbers to make sure that your business makes money after interest, taxes, and depreciation.

How Much Money Will You Make?

Here is a quick table to help you see how much income you might make off your truck. Assuming you own 100 percent of your truck and make consistent revenue about 320 days a year and pay yourself the 10 percent earning, this is what you would make:

$500/day   → $160,000 in revenue → $16,000 in net income

$1000/day → $320,000 in revenue → $32,000 in net income

$2000/day → $640,000 in revenue → $64,000 in net income

$3000/day → $960,000 in revenue → $96,000 in net income

Make It Look Good

If you are looking for investors, you should treat your business plan with the same care and concern as a résumé. Use spell check. Review grammar. Be consistent. Investors will interpret lack of attention to detail as an inability to execute. Print and bind your business plan and include high-quality color photos if you have any images of the truck or the food. Images speak louder than words.

If you are serious enough about your business to write a business plan, you should be serious enough to hire a graphic designer. A logo and a rendering of the truck will make it look a lot more real. If you are on a budget, you can hire a student from a local design school. Also, if you are comfortable working remotely, check out Elance to hire a talented freelance graphic designer.

Raising Money

THE FIRST THING you're going to need to do is raise the money you need to get your business started. Obviously, if you have a lot of cash sitting in a bank account, you are good to go. Otherwise, you're going to need to raise the money. Some of the best ways to go about it are to raise money from friends and family or to crowdsource your funding.

Empty Your Bank Account!

Before you do anything else, try and assemble whatever funds you can yourself. Everyone has their own threshold for risk. Investors are going to look to make sure that you have skin in the game. Obviously, if you think this business is a good enough investment for your time and effort, you should think it is a good investment for your money as well. Any funding you secure from outside sources will dilute your owner-ship in the business. If it is important to you to have full control over the business, you'll want to do what you can to find the money on your own, get small business loans, or max out credit cards. It is also possible to potentially roll over your retirement accounts into a new business. Companies such as as SDCooper, Benetrends, and Guidant Financial provide this service and allow you to avoid early withdrawal fees.

Friends and Family

One source of capital for a small business is from friends and family. These are people who already know you and trust you and have a vested interest in you and seeing you succeed. In order to preserve your relationships with friends and family, you should make sure that you have a paper trail for everything. You should also think carefully about who you ask and how much you ask for. If your venture fails and you are unable to pay back your friends and family, it could have a serious impact on your relationships. Don't underestimate the ability of money to undermine your relationships. It may sound ridiculous, but role-play what a conversation would be like to tell a friend or a family member that you lost their investment. Ask yourself if you are sure the relationship would survive if you couldn't pay back your friend or family member. If you suspect the answer is "no," don't take the money.

Crowdsourcing

Crowdsourcing is a new concept that allows you to raise small amounts of money from a large pool of investors. There are a number of crowdsourcing firms out there, including Prosper, Kickstarter, Rockethub, ProFounder, and IndieGoGo. Once you have your branding done, you should put your concept out on one of these sites with a few "levels" of investment.

$10 for a free meal during opening week

$50 for a branded T-shirt and a free meal during opening week

$100 for an invitation to the opening party, a T-shirt, and a free meal

$1,000 to get a menu item named after you

$5,000 for free meals from the truck for a year

Bank Loans

Bank loans can be hard to get if you don't have an existing business. Many banks are extremely risk averse and require two years of profitable operations before they offer credit. Smaller banks tend to be more flexible, so if you get turned down by a large bank, try a community bank or credit union. If this is your first business, don't take it personally. Keep a dialogue open with the loan officer and try to set a time by which you can prove the operations are successful at which you can get a loan or a letter of credit. Even if you cannot open your first truck on a bank loan, you might be able to open your second truck on one.

Small Business Administration Loans

The Small Business Administration (SBA) backs loans made to small businesses. If a small business defaults, the SBA guarantees up to 85 to 90 percent of the loan. Check the Small Business Administration website to find banks in your area that participate in the SBA loan program. Again, even if you cannot get initial funding for your business, starting a dialogue now for future expansion is a good idea.

Microloans

Microloans are a new concept that have been used successfully in the developing world but also have a place here in the United States. While you will probably only be able to get a few thousand dollars toward your venture, you will probably be able to get reasonable terms as well as mentorship and public relations opportunities. One prominent vendor that does loans in the United States is Accion USA. Accion partners with organizations like Kiva.org, Tory Burch, and Sam Adams. Accion offers specific expertise in hospitality ventures at www.accionusa.org.

Asset-Backed Loans or Leases

While the costs of asset-backed loans or leases are a lot more expensive than a traditional bank loan, if you are strapped for cash, they can be a good way to get started. Some kitchen equipment companies and some food truck manufacturers offer financing as part of their purchasing program.

Professional Investors

Typically, angel investors or venture capital funds are looking for very scalable businesses. Because of some of the operational constraints of food trucks, they are not the right people to talk to if you are planning to open one food truck and live off of the cash. However, if you are planning to open the next fast, casual concept to sweep across the country, you might be able to secure a funding plan to get the money to open a truck, and then a store, and then a group of stores when you hit certain targets at each step along the way. Professional investors will demand a lot more ownership for the money they give you, but they will offer guidance and assistance to help the business succeed in order to protect their investment.

Bootstrapping

Even if you cannot find the money that you need to get started in a truck initially, there are options. If your concept can work on a food truck, maybe you can scale it down a bit and execute it on a food cart. That could cut your start-up costs in half. And if even a cart is initially out of reach, you can start by selling your food on weekends at a farmers' market. Starting small by testing your food out in markets will help you refine the food, learn about operations, and also establish credit history for your business. If you vend profitably for two years in markets, you'll probably have a good case to get a bank loan for a food truck. Many of the most successful trucks in New York City including Coolhaus, Milk Truck NYC, and Red Hook Lobster Pound started vending in markets before moving to trucks.

Start: Making It Happen

ONCE YOU'VE SECURED the money you need, you need to spend it quickly and effectively to get open on time. Getting your truck to market quickly will be an important component in your success. Many restaurants fail during the opening process because of poor planning that causes delays. Since they aren't earning revenue, they can burn through their cash cushion before even opening. Because food trucks have less overhead, it is harder for this to happen, but delays or poor planning can cut into your working capital and limit your flexibility for future problems or push your opening from the peak of high season into the doldrums of a low season. The next several chapters are focused on the steps you need to get your truck open and ready for business.

Administrative Necessities

Create an Office Space

Any business, even a food truck, generates a lot of paperwork. In order to stay organized, you should set aside some physical space in your home or existing business as an office. Even a small nook will do. You'll need a place to organize incoming bills, process your weekly paperwork, and keep the administrative aspects of your office organized. You should also have a small file cabinet to keep your important business records.

One piece of office equipment that will make a huge difference in your quality of life is a scanner. A scanner will give you the ability to get paper documents into your computer where you can more easily access them remotely. One scanner to take a look at is the Fujitsu S1500.

Set Up a Virtual Office

Because you will be on the move all the time in your truck, it will be extremely helpful for you to set up a virtual office as well. Having a good way to get access to important documents remotely is extremely important in this business. You may be contacted by a banker about a loan application just as you are pulling into your commissary in the afternoon, so being able to access the paperwork remotely could be very helpful. Set up a system to file important files on your computer. Some services that are very helpful for backing up and accessing documents remotely on "the cloud" from a laptop or a computer include Dropbox (dropbox.com) or Egnyte (egnyte.com).

Set Up a Legal Entity

There are a number of ways you can organize your business. Some of the most common ways are as a sole proprietorship, a partnership, a limited liability company (LLC), an S Corp, or a C Corp. Each has different legal and tax consequences. Some of the key considerations are taxation, personal liability, and administrative costs. You should take the time to investigate the consequences of each with your lawyer and your accountant.

Once you have set up your business, you will need to register for an employer identification number (EIN) with the IRS (www.irs.gov). As soon as you have an EIN, you should start applying for all the permits and licenses you'll need to legally operate. In some states you may be required to show proof of insurance to obtain health permits or register your food truck, so setting up your insurance coverage early will be important as well.

Getting Insurance

Running a food truck is a very risky business, and insurance helps you hedge against that risk. Even if you run your truck to the highest standards of cleanliness and safety, something could go wrong outside of your control that could jeopardize the future of your business. You should insure your business adequately so that even if something catastrophic happens to your truck, you can protect your investors and your business. If you want to dig into the nuances of insuring your food truck, please take a look at the following blog by Matthew Carlson, who is a VP at Risk Strategies Company, a company that has specific insurance products for food trucks: cateringtruckinsurance.blogspot.com.

- **Liability insurance:** A solid base package of coverage for one truck would be $2,000,000 in general liability insurance, $1,000,000 max per occurrence, and $1,000,000 in products liability insurance. Get insurance that allows you to list additional insured entities for free. If you plan on vending on private property, public property, or doing special events, find out what the normal insurance requirements are in your city so that you get sufficient insurance. Many properties will require you to name them on your insurance policy. If you plan on doing a lot of special events, make sure to get a policy that doesn't charge you extra to list additionally insured entities.

- **Auto insurance:** While you may be able to get your food truck insured in your own name, it is a good idea to get a commercial auto insurance policy with $500,000 to $1,000,000 in liability insurance. Be sure to provide your insurer with the names and driver's license identification numbers for anyone on your team who will be driving the truck so they will be covered. Most food truck insurance claims are related to automobile liability.
- **Workman's compensation** and **disability insurance:** You should check to see if this coverage is required by law in your state.

There are a number of great insurance brokers out there. Talk with a few to see how you like them. Ask about how they handle claims, about the turn-around time for repairs, and whether you can use your own mechanic for repairs or if you need to use a specific insurance company-approved mechanic. While you can work with anyone, there are a number of vendors who specialize in insuring food trucks. Two companies you might want to take a look at are Risk Strategies Company (risk-strategies.com) and Whorton (whortonins.com).

Apply for Licenses

If there are long waiting lists or the application process is time consuming, be sure to start with enough time to get your truck open in time.

Don't forget to get the appropriate vehicle permits and licenses from your state's department of motor vehicles for your food truck. In all likelihood, you will need commercial plates for your truck, so the process might be slightly different from what you are used to for your personal vehicle.

Set Up Your Systems

Before you hit the streets, you'll definitely want a few core systems set up so your business will be organized.

- **Finances:** Your accountant can help you set up a basic financial system to do the following: pay bills, reconcile deposits, manage petty cash, and pay sales tax. You'll probably also want to create an invoice template to invoice clients if you plan to do catering or special events.

- **Filing:** Aside from important business documents, you'll need to set aside space to archive financial documents. Financial documents need to be kept for three to seven years, depending on the types of documents.
- **Cash management:** Food trucks tend to do a lot of business in cash. Cash has a way of disappearing if you don't keep a close eye on it. You'll need to start every shift with lots of singles so you can make change for large bills. And at the end of each day, you'll want to store your cash someplace safe. If you have room in your truck, install a drop safe. Direct Safes (directsafes.com) is a good source for drop safes. If you have a bank that will accept night deposits, that is the best resource; however, if not, you'll need to work out the details of where your cash is located and create a system to make sure it is accounted for. If you cannot fit a drop safe on your truck, you should definitely have one at your commissary.
- **Maintenance:** Food trucks break down, but before they break down, small things start to go awry. Developing a process to track those small issues and address them before they develop into large problems can dramatically improve the profitability of your business. Talk with your truck fabricator, your equipment manufacturers, your generator manufacturer, and your mechanic about preventive maintenance. Schedule it ahead of time, and don't miss the appointments. Keep all of these appointments scheduled in one central calendar, such as Google calendar. This will ensure you don't miss any scheduled maintenance, which would invariably lead to unnecessary breakdowns.

Cash Registers versus Point of Sales Systems (POS)

You will need a system to manage your cash. Many municipalities require you to provide receipts for all commercial transactions, so having a cash register is a good idea. When choosing how to manage cash, a few important decision criteria to keep in mind are:

- Stability (doesn't break down on its own)
- Durability (sturdy enough to survive on a truck—iPads probably need cases)
- Speed of service (doesn't get in the way of a transaction)

- Ability to get at useful data
- Support for tech challenges
- TCO (total cost of ownership): is it affordable?

Registers are tried and true. They tend to get high marks for stability and durability, but they can be challenging to program and to get accurate reports from. While many POS systems built for restaurants are too robust and too expensive to be used on a food truck, there has been a lot of innovation in tablet POS systems. If you can afford it, a cloud-based POS system on a handheld tablet or a laptop might hit the sweet spot. Two iPad-based systems worth taking a look at are Revelsystems .com and Shopkeep.com.

Credit Cards

Cash is common currency for street foods. Customers expect to pay in cash, so if you don't offer to take credit cards, it doesn't really hurt your business. However, customers tend to spend a bit more freely when using credit. Your average check might be a $1 or $2 higher on credit card purchases compared to cash. The only downside is the merchant services fees that credit card companies charge.

Even if you don't accept credit cards for street vending, you should set up an account with a merchant services provider so that you can get paid for catering or special events via credit card. Some customers will prefer to pay by credit card rather than check. A simple way to accept credit cards for special events is by setting up an account with Paypal or Square (Squareup.com). With Paypal you can run credit cards over the Internet. Square lets you run credit cards from a smartphone and offers discounts if you swipe the card.

If you opt to take credit for street vending, you should test the system for stability and speed of service. Look at point-of-sale credit card equipment and peripherals by VeriFone, Nurit, Hypercom, Way Systems, Exadigm, Authorize.net, and Magtek. Some major merchant services companies include Authorize.net. Be sure to shop around for the best prices based on your level of volume. There are a number of start-ups working on payment processing via mobile phones. This could be very interesting for food truck operators because the transactions are quick and don't require extra hardware. One company that has been successful in Boston and Philadelphia and is making inroads in New York City is TheLevelUp.com.

Foundational Paperwork

No one likes paperwork, but by planning your operations before you get started, you'll be much more organized and better able to attend to the real work of your business: selling great food to your customers. Once you do the big push to get your business set up, you should work on planning out your operations on paper while your fabricator is building out the truck.

Descriptions of the types of documents you might want to prepare to keep your business organized are listed next.

Resources

- **Credit sheet:** A one-page document that has all the critical information that vendors need to get you set up in their accounts. This should include your business's legal name, mailing address, delivery address, contact info, bank information, and credit references.
- **Important numbers:** A short document that has the contact information for all the important vendors that keep your business running smoothly. You'll definitely want your mechanic, truck fabricator, and commissary listed here. You should also find a towing service that can tow a vehicle the size of your truck in an emergency. All your food and beverage vendors as well as your insurance broker should be on this list.
- **Schedule template and staff list:** You'll want your schedule to be organized in a way that is easy for your team members to figure out when they are working, and everyone should have the contact information for everyone else so that they can arrange coverage if it's needed. One amazing innovation in scheduling technology in the past few years has been the development of very robust online scheduling services. Take a look at Schedulefly.com, Whentomanage .com, or Hotschedules.com.
- **Truck paperwork binder:** Start assembling a binder for your truck that has copies of all of the relevant permits and licenses for your business and your truck. If you ever get inspected, you'll want to

have all of these things handy. Buy plastic sleeves for your documents. This makes it easy to get them in and out in a hurry and also keeps them protected from food or beverage spills.

HR Forms

- **Application:** Before you start hiring, it is a good idea to have an application. There are lots of great examples of these online.
- **New-hire packet:** Once you decide to add someone to your team, you'll need to collect a lot of information and keep it organized. It may help you to premake packets that include the legally required paperwork like W-4 and I-9 forms as well as any additional information you might want to collect, such as emergency contact information or a nondisclosure, noncompete agreement. Basic training materials like the menu and contact information are good to share initially as well.
- **Policy manual:** In order to protect yourself from potential lawsuits, you should assemble a policy manual that has relevant rules and regulations for your state. While most policy manuals end up being a rather large collection of commonsense rules, such as don't bring your pet to work, they exist because sometimes your employees may not use common sense and it gives you a legal foundation to enforce rules.
- **Expectations and obligations:** Because a policy manual can get very dense and bulky, it is a good idea to have a one-page document that clearly spells out your exact expectations of your employees and your obligations to them as an employer. If you want people to be in uniform before they clock in, let them know. At a basic minimum, this document should stress the importance of timeliness and communication. Both of these attributes are essential to the smooth operation of a mobile food operation.

Operational Forms

- **Order sheet:** Food trucks need food. The order sheet will help you organize your purchasing and ensure that whatever you order arrives. The order sheet should contain all the items you routinely purchase. Usually it is easiest to organize by vendor. When you place an order, mark on the sheet what day you expect it to arrive. When the orders arrive, check the physical goods dropped off against the invoice and the original order.

- **Time sheets:** Unless you have a POS that can track when your staff log in and log out or some other time and attendance solution, you'll need time sheets to track hours. Something basic with name, start time, end time, and total hours should be sufficient.
- **Daily sales sheet:** You'll need paperwork to track the sales each day. Your sales paperwork should reconcile the cash that is turned in at the end of the shift to sales from your register or POS system. If you are doing purchases from cash, you should be able to account for petty cash. If you sell a product that is easy to inventory, it is a good idea to tie out your inventory changes to sales. For instance, if you sell pretzels for $5 each and you started the day with 25 pretzels and have 5 left at the end, you should have collected $100. To do that, you'll need to track opening and closing inventory as well as any discards during the shift.
- **Daily log:** The daily log should track important details about each day's operation. Red Book Solutions (bettermanagers.com) has a great product that is used in many restaurants that can easily be adjusted for use in a food truck, or you could make your own. Be sure to track basics like the day, the weather, and who is working each shift as well as important operational details such as staff notes, customer feedback, food quality, cleaning projects, and maintenance.
- **Cash management forms:** In order to have accountability in your cash management process, it might help to have sheets to track the start of your drawer as well as your safe. You will also want a form to track bank deposits.

Training Materials

- **Job descriptions:** Written job descriptions help employees understand what will be asked of them. Make requirements clear. Operating a food truck often involves a bit of physical labor for loading and unloading the trucks, so make sure your employees can lift what is required. Also, if driving (is a special drivers license required?) is a prerequisite, make sure they know.

■ **Recipes:** Reproducible recipes will keep your food consistent.

■ **Line manual:** This is a document that "shows" what all of your products look like when ready to be served for guests. Take photos of all your dishes properly prepared with correct garnishes and por-tioned properly in the correct container. Print this document in color and have it on the truck to refer to when training so you can ensure your products are always coming out consistently.

■ **Menu descriptions:** Write out key speaking points about every item on the menu so your staff can describe them fluently.

■ **Daily checklists:** These should track the major responsibilities for daily operations including what to do before you leave the com-missary, setting up before service, closing up on-site, and closing at the commissary.

■ **Weekly checklists:** Track weekly responsibilities, usually related to cleaning or maintenance.

■ **Monthly checklists:** Track monthly responsibilities, which are usually related to maintenance or bookkeeping. This is also a good way to track oil changes and tune-ups for both the truck and the generator. Take a thorough inventory monthly for your accountant.

Finalizing the Menu

IT's TIME TO refine the menu you drafted for your business plan. Your goal is to come up with a menu that is fun and enjoyable for your customers but also practical and efficient. Before you spec out your truck, you need to have a good idea of the depth and scope of your menu so that you can build a truck that can accommodate everything that you want to sell. For excellent tips on designing and pricing your menu, refer to *Menu Pricing and Strategy* by Jack Miller and David Pavesic.

Often menu development is an iterative process as you work through your desired menu, the desired size of truck, and the generator or power source you plan to use. If your menu is very broad, you may need to get a larger truck and a larger generator, which can increase your budget.

Keep Constraints in Mind

Usually, there is a bit of an iterative process as the menu is drafted and refined in regard to the practicalities of operating off of a truck. The major constraints to be mindful of as you home your menu are limited space and limited power. The lack of space on a food truck has several consequences. First, there isn't much storage space for a wide variety of items, so it helps to have prep ingredients that can be stored efficiently and used in multiple recipes. Also, there isn't much prep space. The lack of power means you may have to pick and choose from a limited amount of kitchen equipment to prepare your dishes. You may end up having to do a lot of different dishes on one piece of equipment, which can slow up your operations.

Choosing Menu Items

In general, a focused menu is preferable, because you want to be able to execute well with all the items on your menu. However, at the same time, there needs to be some variety to bring in repeat customers. Also, consider how customers buy. A good foundational menu mix for a savory truck might be three entrees, three sides, and three drinks.

First and foremost, menu items should be consistent with the brand and valuable to the customers. Menu items should also be affordable with a COGS of less than 30 percent including the cost of packaging. They should be fast to serve, and they should fit within the equipment constraints. Another important consideration is the shelf-life of the raw ingredients.

Picking Vendors

Finding reliable vendors with good pricing is a big challenge. A big challenge for food trucks is hitting order minimums for major purveyors. National food-service purveyors like Sysco or US Foods often have minimums that will be too high for a single food truck unless you have a lot of storage space. Because you are mobile, you can drive to food-service supply stores like Restaurant Depot or Jetro, or use national wholesalers like Costco or Sam's Club.

When picking vendors, you want to get the best quality product for the lowest price. However, don't underestimate the importance of credit. If a vendor has slightly more expensive product but will give you 45 days of term instead of COD, it might be worth it. For anything expensive, or for items with the highest velocity, get pricing from multiple vendors.

Buy Local

Local and sustainable food is great for the environment and one of the hottest trends in food. In addition to being socially responsible, it has great marketing cache. Food trucks are well positioned to capitalize on this growing trend. Because food trucks tend to buy in smaller quantities, they can source directly from local farmers. Also, without the cost of rent, food trucks can invest more value in high-quality ingredients for their products. While finding local food growers can be a challenge, a number of services exist to assist farmers in finding customers for their locally produced food in urban markets. In New York City and surrounding areas, take a look at Basis Foods (farmtochefnyc.com).

Recipes

In order to get your food made consistently and correctly, you'll need to get your recipes out of your head and onto paper. Be sure to make your recipes very specific. Having your prep team add pepper to taste will be inconsistent over time as everyone has different taste. It is better to determine a specific amount of pepper. Convert recipes to be done by weight instead of by volume. When products ship, they tend to settle and, depending on how densely packed they are, the amount in a cup can change slightly. Recipes done by weight will give you more consistency and are easier to scale, especially if you move to a copacker as you grow in the future.

Food Costing

Take the time to figure out food costs for all your items before you open. Once you open, it will be a lot harder to find the time to do these calculations. However, knowing your food costs on specific items will give you the knowledge you need to determine pricing and which items deserve to stay on the menu over time.

Pricing

There are several methods of pricing including cost pricing, competitive-based pricing, or value pricing. Cost pricing is pricing based on the cost of a good to supply. Competitive-based pricing is pricing based on how others in the market are pricing. Value pricing is based on the value of the offering. To the extent possible, you will want to do value pricing, but make sure your costs are covered and you are priced competitively against other food vendors. In order to get ready to price your menu, you should do some research to see what prices other vendors are charging for goods of similar quality. Can you compete at that price? Some restaurants may be able to have prices that are more competitive than you might anticipate. If a restaurant is in a below-market lease, they might have lower occupancy costs than you'd expect. Nationally chained restaurants might be able to get better pricing because of the large volume of business they do with food-service suppliers. Incorporating sales tax into the price of your items will make your transactions much faster. Rounding to the nearest quarter saves you time making change. Leave the dimes, nickels, and pennies at home.

Lay Out Your Kitchen

ONCE YOU HAVE a high degree of confidence that you have the menu you are planning to open with, you can work on laying out your kitchen. Some food truck fabricators sell predesigned trucks, so you will be adjusting an existing layout. Others can manage the entire kitchen design in-house. Still others will ask that you provide the layout for them to build. While this section will be most relevant to entrepreneurs who are going to custom-build the kitchen on the bed of their truck, even if you are buying or renting a prefabricated truck, you should take some time to consider the layout of your kitchen and how it might be improved to increase speed of service.

Keep Constraints in Mind

Because your kitchen will be built onto the back of a truck, it is important to keep in mind that the width and length of your line will be limited. The widest food trucks are about 86 inches, so the width of the line is fixed. Step vans generally have beds that start at 10 feet in length and then grow in two-foot increments. If you don't have a truck already, there is a bit of iteration as you will try out different configurations of equipment layout and the space you'll require. If you are trying to fit into the specs of a specific truck body, you should have the interior dimensions of that space handy, including any features you need to design around. Don't forget about the wheel wells of the step van!

Also, design your truck with mobility in mind. If you are doing street vending or might need to vend at multiple sites per day, you need to consider the time that will be required to set up. There is a coffee vendor at my old depot who used to come in at 3 AM to light his coffee urn

82

and then go home to sleep two more hours before taking his cart out in the morning. If you are selling savory food and have a fryer, you'll want to consider a way to safely drain the hot oil out before driving.

Don't Freehand It

On a food truck, every inch counts. It is important to do the layout of the space to scale. Ideally this would be done in a computer-aided design (CAD) program. If you don't have the software to do this, you can lay out your truck carefully to scale on graph paper. It might also be worth hiring a kitchen equipment specialist to help you lay out the truck and choose the equipment. Many food truck fabricators will do the truck design with you or for you. Oftentimes this is the best solution, as they will know the local rules and regulations pertaining to truck design. Once you have finalized the design of your truck, be sure to take the blueprints for approval from the appropriate agency. Even if it isn't required to get sign-off, it is helpful to avoid problems that might materialize down the line. It is much more expensive to rebuild a truck than to adjust a design, so if there is going to be a problem, it behooves you catch it as soon as possible.

Design for Speed of Service

As you block out the space, think about the roles for each of the members of the team that will be working the truck. If you are selling cupcakes this is pretty simple because generally you will have one person working who can ring up orders and hand out cupcakes. If you are selling burgers or tacos and you have a team of three or four people working the truck at the same time, things can get very crowded very quickly. If there is a grill man, an expediter, and a cashier, it is likely that each of them will be relatively locked into their positions, so the grill man needs access to the refrigerator that holds the proteins that he'll be grilling. The expediter will need access to storage for paper products and prepped vegetables. Think about how information will be communicated to everyone on the team. Some trucks just call out orders. But it is good practice to have a ticket lineup. One challenge may be that only a few employees will be in a position to see the tickets. Be sure to set aside space for trash cans.

Service Window (or Windows)

As you lay out the line, think about where you would put a service window. It will probably need to go somewhere in the middle of the line, but it need not necessarily be exactly in the middle. Generally, your service window will be on the passenger side of the vehicle. However, if you are planning on doing street vending, you might benefit from having windows on both sides of the truck so you can vend to pedestrians when parked on either side of the street. Incorporating two service windows into the design will probably cost you some storage and you'll need to save space to move your register or point of sales system from one side of the truck to the other if necessary. Also, consider the height of the curb when you think about where your window will be. Curbs in your city might give customers a six- to eight-inch boost to bring them closer to the action.

Picking Equipment

Key considerations for equipment on food trucks include the size, power requirements, and cooking/cooling power. Because food trucks are narrow, you'll have to find kitchen equipment that is a bit narrower than what is used in most restaurants.

One thing to keep in mind when choosing equipment is that the use of the equipment on a mobile vehicle may void the warranty. The constant shaking and rattling of being on a truck can be hard on kitchen equipment that was designed to operate in the safe stability of a restaurant. Check with the manufacturer and ask if their warranty is valid on a truck. I am hoping that as more professional operators participate in mobile food, manufacturers will develop more durable equipment specifically for the mobile work environment.

The equipment you choose will ultimately dictate the size of the generator that is required to power your truck. The more power-intensive your equipment is, the larger the generator you'll require. You should keep a spreadsheet that summarizes the amps and voltage of each piece of equipment so you know the maximum load that the truck might need.

Make sure that all your equipment is installed in a way where it is secure. A good practice is to work with your fabricator to install latches to fasten down all of the equipment securely. Think about what the kitchen looks like in the last flight you took. The flight attendants have these amazing clips that hold everything down. You'll want that same feature. Nothing will be more frustrating than taking a corner a bit too fast and watching the contents of your fridge pour out onto the floor when the refrigerator door swings open.

When you have the final kitchen equipment chosen, take pains to have it installed in a way that you can move it in order to clean. Narrow gaps attract all sorts of trouble. Kitchen equipment should be sealed in or have the ability to be moved so you can clean. Ensure that the installation locations for your kitchen equipment allow for proper ventilation.

As a final note, the number one regret I hear all the time from truck owners once their truck is built is not having incorporated more refrigeration. Think through your menu mix carefully. If you have room to spare, add another fridge. The one bit of solace is that after the build, if you're desperate for fridge space, you can always put soda and bottled water in a cooler with ice.

Water and Power

Just as if you were going to build a brick-and-mortar restaurant, you need to be mindful of the core utilities. Know all of the regulatory requirements for the size of your water and wastewater tanks and the size sink that you'll need. In some cases you may need only a hand sink, but in others you may need a two-compartment sink. Don't forget to include space for a hot-water heater and a pump if you'll need it for running water. Think about the location of the fuse box and where you'll need outlets. I'd recommend building out for a bit of extra capacity in case you want to add small pieces of kitchen equipment on the counter in the future.

Consider the type of shoreline you'll use to power the fridges on your truck overnight. As more and more trucks move from stable to vending, vending locations open up the possibility to power the truck by shoreline instead of by generator. Being able to easily get enough power to the onboard system to power the whole truck is essential to make the best use of these systems. Many electric vehicle charging stations use a J1772 connector, so using this connector or being able to convert to it may be useful in the future.

HVAC

Yes, you definitely need to consider your heating, venting, and air conditioning. If you're cooking, in most cases you'll need some sort of venting system for the exhaust. Depending on the climate, you may want to consider an AC unit. Mobile AC units often require a fair amount of power and may not be effective at keeping your truck cool if you are doing a lot of cooking. Fans will be very important. Make sure you have exhaust fans on the roof to let the heat escape.

Test Your Kitchen before You Build It

Find an open space someplace in your garage or your basement and lay out your theoretical kitchen to scale. Get a tape measure and some masking tape and tape out the measurements of the bed of the truck. If possible, arrange furniture that is roughly the size of the equipment you'll be using in the space. Assemble a group of as many people as you expect to be working at a time in the truck and then bring one extra to act as a customer. Practice doing orders to make sure everyone has the room they need to get their work done and to get at the equipment and products they need to be successful.

Role-play the following scenarios:

- Order everything off of the menu in different combinations.
- Restock food.
- Restock paper.
- Throw away trash.

Procuring a Truck

BUILDING OUT A truck is one of the more frightening and exciting parts of developing your business. As with every other step, take time to plan ahead. Double-check to make sure your truck is in compliance with local regulations. Some key details to investigate include the permissible length of vehicles and the required amount of freshwater and wastewater storage. Certain markets like Los Angeles have very strict construction codes.

Rent or Build

The first big decision will be whether to rent a food truck or build your own. In some markets there isn't the option of renting, so the choice will be made for you. If there is the opportunity to rent a food truck, it is an option worth considering. In certain markets, like Los Angeles, the majority of trucks are leased. In other markets, like New York City, almost all the trucks are built to spec.

For some companies, leasing a prefabricated catering truck for the long term may make more sense. The primary advantage is a lower capital outlay. Leasing also typically provides the food truck with a place to park at night and routine maintenance. On the downside, the truck will not be customized to the company's specifications, so this wouldn't work for a company with very specific needs, such as a dessert truck or pizza truck. But for a company that needs only the basic kitchen supplies (griddle, deep fryer, oven), leasing may be a good solution. Leasing a truck typically costs $2,000 to $4,000 per month. Companies that lease food trucks include MobiMunch (mobimunch .com/leasing) and RoadStoves (roadstoves.com).

Picking a Truck

If you decide to build your own truck, the first big purchase will be the truck itself. There are many criteria to consider, including the bed size of the truck, design of the truck, and the condition of the truck.

Bed Size

Before looking at trucks, you should have a very good idea of the kitchen size you are working with. The smallest step vans usually have a 10-foot bed. The bed is increased in 2-foot increments, so 12-foot, 14-foot, and 16-foot beds are all common. A food truck fabricator can help you lay out a kitchen in your truck. When you are laying out the kitchen, pay close attention to the location of wheel wells and the height of the back of the truck. It is generally a bad idea to buy a truck and then try to fit your kitchen into it.

Truck Type

Many food trucks are built on a step van chassis. Step vans are commonly used as bread or snack delivery trucks. The big advantage of step vans is that the beds are lower to the ground, so servers aren't too far away from customers who are ordering from the sidewalk. Step van styles that you can search for on Craigslist include: Chevrolet P30, Ford P30, Ford E350, Freightliner MT45, GMC P30, Grumman Olson, Utilimaster, or Workhorse W42. Used step vans typically cost $5,000 to $20,000 depending on the condition of the vehicle. New step vans cost $40,000 to $70,000. Isuzu started production of a step van called the Reach in 2011, which costs around $60,000. If you have a slim menu and you can fit into a narrower vehicle, the Dodge Sprinter is a good option. The Sprinter is a good alternative because it is easier to drive and park than a step van, which might be a big advantage in a city where parking is scarce.

Truck Condition

Buy a truck in the best condition you can afford. Buying a 20-year-old truck to save a thousand dollars on your start-up costs is going to cost you tens of thousands of dollars down the road in maintenance and, more important, it can cost you lost revenue. Every day that your truck is broken down and in the shop is a day that you aren't on the road earning revenue. Used trucks may seem like they make a lot of sense when you are on a tight budget getting started. However, consider the long term. Find a mechanic you trust and bring him or her with you to test out each truck you consider. Make sure that expensive items like the engine and the transmission are in good repair. One good way to find a used step van is at auction. USPS, UPS, FedEx, and the US Military all use step vans and take very good care of their fleet vehicles. Step vans decommissioned from a professionally managed fleet tend to be in better shape than those owned by individuals.

Fuel Type

This decision can be made in large part by the price of gasoline or diesel in your city. However, there are a few other factors to consider including engine life, mileage, and the availability of good mechanics. Diesel engines generally last longer and require less regular maintenance. Anecdotally, an engine might last 50 to 75 percent longer, but it really depends on the upkeep. However, if you have a problem with the fuel delivery system, it is more complex than a gasoline engine and therefore more expensive to fix. Gasoline has better acceleration, but diesel engines offer more torque, so they are usually better suited to powering heavy trucks or vans. Because food trucks never go very fast but start and stop a lot, that torque translates into better fuel efficiency from diesel trucks. My mechanic told me that diesel is estimated to be about 20 percent better. One downside to diesel for those with food trucks in cold environments is that a diesel engine can sludge up in the winter. From an ecological perspective, diesel is slightly better for the environment. First, diesel engines can be run on biodiesel fuel. Cooking oil can be converted to biodiesel, so there is something poetic about dropping off used cooking oil and then filling up with biodiesel. Also, diesel fuel produces larger particulates in the exhaust produced. These particulates tend to fall out of the atmosphere quicker and are less likely to be absorbed into the blood system.

Eco-Friendly Options

Many businesses are looking to incorporate environmentally responsible business practices into the construction and ongoing operation of their businesses. It is important to be thoughtful and make sure environmentally friendly practices are operationally effective as well as socially responsible. The easiest concession for a food truck operator is to use biodiesel.

If you're feeling a bit more adventurous you can convert a truck to be powered by compressed natural gas, like The Treats Truck in New York City. However, be sure you have a mechanic you really trust because when you make serious changes to an engine, you're committing to a special relationship with your mechanic.

There are a few step vans that are powered by hybrid engines. If you are interested in a hybrid step van, many of the major manufacturers, such as Freightliner, are experimenting with this technology. Also, there are a few manufacturers who are specifically building hybrids for the trucking market, like Azure Dynamics (azuredynamics.com), which has a hybrid step van engine, which purports to reduce fuel expenses by 40 percent, maintenance costs by 30 percent, and emissions by 30 percent. Hybrids are great for improving fuel efficiency while you are driving, but many food trucks aren't driven that far on a daily basis, so your savings might not offset the higher costs of the initial purchase of a hybrid step van. Also, the batteries that are used to power the truck when it is running off of electricity are all stowed below the chassis, where food trucks need space for water tanks and generators, so fully test your ability to lay out your kitchen on a hybrid.

There are a few electric trucks out there suitable to be built into food trucks, such as the Isuzu Zero (isuzu.com) or Smith Edison (smithelectric.com). In 2011, Freightliner just came out with an all-electric step van built off of their MT-45 chassis. Because the technology for electric vehicles is still new, these trucks are very expensive, usually costing about $150,000 for a new truck. Also, like hybrids, the batteries take up quite a bit of space on the undercarriage. Unless you are running a truck with very low power requirements that can be run off a battery, you will probably need to use a generator. While eliminating the responsibility of paying for gasoline is thrilling, these trucks have a limited operating radius of about 100 miles, so be sure you won't be using your truck to commute large distances. Be wary of electric trucks that don't go at least 55 mph, and pay close attention to the weight loads that these trucks can carry.

Many states and even some large municipalities offer tax credits or rebates for incorporating eco-friendly fuel sources or equipment into your design. If this is something you are planning to incorporate into your operation, be sure you check to see if there are financial incentives to help cover the upfront investment costs.

Power

Food trucks need power to operate. Just about every truck requires a generator to have electricity for basic necessities, but if you are cooking, you can choose how to power your kitchen equipment as well as your generator.

Kitchen equipment can be run off of natural gas or propane. Propane has historically been the fuel of choice for cooking because it is inexpensive, readily available, and very energy dense. It is lightweight, quiet, and eco-friendly. It can be used to cook, power generators, and even run refrigeration units. Propane is also very reliable. Because there are very few moving parts involved, trucks hardly ever lose a day of operations due to a problem with their propane system. However, propane is extremely combustible, which can be quite a liability if it isn't managed properly.

If you grill meats or have an energy-intensive cooking process, you may require the cooking power of propane or natural gas for your griddle or grill. However, if you can manage without, it is worth considering leaving the propane tanks at home. While it is less efficient, powering your equipment off of a diesel or gasoline generator is much simpler and safer. Having one energy source means only one tank of fuel to fill (if you run your generator off your fuel tank.) Also, propane can be very dangerous if not handled correctly. If the propane isn't secured before driving, it can cause a terrible accident.

One exciting advantage of a truck that can be powered completely by electricity is the possibility of vending indoors. Propane is generally not permitted for use indoors because burning propane releases carbon monoxide. While many food trucks might never come across this opportunity, if there is a big indoor venue, you can get access to doing private events or indoor catering where other trucks might not be able to. If you plan to use propane, try to incorporate the ability to operate solely off of electricity. It might come in handy.

There are a number of criteria to think about when choosing a generator, including wattage, price, noise, fuel type, size, and postpurchase service.

- **Generator wattage:** To determine the watts needed, add up the wattage (volts × amps) necessary for all appliances being run simultaneously. Sources suggest adding an overage of at least 15 percent to 20 percent to ensure adequate power.
- **Fuel source:** Generators are made that run off of propane, gas, or diesel. Generally, the easiest thing to do is use whatever fuel is already on your truck. Choose a model that lets you run off of the fuel from your vehicle's fuel tanks. Gasoline generators tend to be a bit less expensive, a bit lighter, and smaller than other fuel types. However, they have shorter life spans and require more maintenance. Diesel generators are the most common model used in commercial environments. Diesel generators are usually more fuel-efficient and require less maintenance. Many models can accommodate biodiesel. Unfortunately, diesel generators are usually more expensive and diesel smoke smells a bit more than gasoline smoke. Also, if you are vending in the wintertime, you may need to add certain additives to work in below-freezing environments. Propane fuel causes fewer carbon emissions and is the most environmentally friendly option. A properly functioning propane model causes no carbon monoxide emissions, but propane is the least efficient fuel source. Eco-friendly alternative generators (such as solar-powered) are available, although they typically cannot handle the power needed by a food truck. If you're interested in looking at solar power, take a look at SunRnr.com and MySolarBackup.com.
- **Price:** A number of manufacturers build generators that can be used on food trucks including Baldor, Briggs & Stratton, Cummins Onan, Generac, Honda, Kubota, Subaru, Voltmaster, Winco, and Yamaha. Honda generators are often recommended by many in the food truck business. Generators can cost anywhere from $500 to $10,000 depending on the power requirements of your kitchen. Generators can also be bought used (propane and diesel

models, as gasoline generators typically do not last as long) for less expense from online sources such as USPowerCo.com and GeneratorSales.com.

- **Service:** For me, the most important criteria for a generator is the postpurchase support. Find where approved mechanics are located and short-list only those vendors who have mechanics that are nearby. Visit their facility and see how responsive they are. Talk to other owners and ask them how good the service is.

- **Wireless remote start:** Some "deluxe" models come equipped with a remote start option. However, this option can also be installed for about $300 to $500 after purchasing the generator by purchasing a separate kit from the company that manufactures the generator.

- **Sound insulation:** Several types of sound blocking/sound absorbing materials are available to reduce the noise of the generators. Many people also choose to create their own soundproofing case for their generators by building a fiberboard box lined with soundproofing insulation or a soundproofing mat. Another option for the box material is "homasote," a recycled soundproofing material (www.homasote.com). Precautions need to be taken to properly ventilate the box in order to prevent overheating or fume buildup, and depending on the type of generator, an exhaust pipe or fan may also be necessary. Many online manuals are available to help people build their own soundproofing boxes.

Finishing Touches: Painting and Wraps

Your customers are going to make a snap judgment about your business based on the way that your truck looks, so it is important to make sure the exterior of the truck looks great. I'd highly recommend working with a graphic designer to come up with a design that captures key elements of your brand and then working with professionals to execute that design. You can get your truck painted, wrapped, or painted with vinyl stickers. Personally, I am a big fan of a painted truck with vinyl stickers. I think it is the most flexible, durable, and cost-effective solution.

Some operators are reticent to do this as occasionally corporate sponsors will buy out a truck and wrap it to promote an event. The wrap can ruin the vinyl stickers. However, it is rare that you'll be asked to wrap your truck for an event. And if you are, usually the sponsor will have a budget to reapply the original stickers on your truck.

Painting

There are a number of websites that explain how to paint a car yourself. You might be tempted to, but if you don't have the experience, I'd highly recommend paying a professional. Call your local paint stores. If a new outfit has opened recently, you might be able to work something out for a few hundred dollars. Maaco has operations almost everywhere and is good to call for a price comp. Getting a step van painted by Maaco might cost you around $1,500. Try to find someone who has a paint booth large enough to fit your entire truck inside.

Wraps

Vehicle wrapping is also known as vehicle graphics, transit graphics, wrap advertising, transit advertising, and vehicle decals. Wraps are a quick and effective way to brand your truck. The wrap is made of a vinyl film that is printed and applied by a truck wrapping company or a general printing company. Materials available include cast vinyl or calendared vinyl.

Cast vinyl is much more durable and can last several years. Cast vinyl can stretch and conform to the curves of your truck better. It is generally recommended for truck wraps due to its durability and better appearance on a curved surface such as a vehicle. However, it is more expensive. Brands of cast vinyl include 3M, Avery, Vector, FDC, and Oracal.

Calendared vinyl is less durable and typically lasts for as long as a few months. It is recommended for short-term displays but not typically recommended for a vehicle wrap unless it is being placed only on the flat sides of something like a box truck (as it does not conform as well around curves). While this is less expensive, it will not last long enough for a typical food truck season. However, it might be useful to use for decals on your truck for short-term promotions or for a menu display.

One way to limit your budget is to paint your truck and then apply decals on the truck using calendared vinyl. While it may not look as polished, it will save you some money, and if your truck is scraped, you'll need to replace only the specific decal that is damaged.

Interview 3: Randy Miller, Vice President of Sales at MobiMunch, on Food Truck Rentals

MobiMunch (mobimunch.com) was founded in 2009. The company is in the process of creating a national food truck rental platform. MobiMunch offers prefabricated food trucks for long-term rental.

Q: How does the MobiMunch platform work?

Basically, we purchase trucks, we recondition them, and we get them ready to go out on the road. So we repair the engines or the transmissions or the kitchen equipment, whatever needs to be fixed up. In some cases we purchase new trucks that were built from scratch. And basically, we rent them out to operators. So obviously there's a cost to financing these trucks, there's a lot of capital investment in these trucks, particularly ours because we go for newer model or brand new trucks and really get them up to a level where they're in very good condition. And instead of having to pay all of that expense yourself, you rent it over time, and the goal is hopefully to make money off the rent payment, and it's a much lower capital investment way to get started.

Q: So you need less money to start in the first place and hopefully you make a profit more quickly.

Exactly right. And also, you have only a 12-month commitment, so if everything goes wrong and it doesn't go well, you have a stop-loss. If you buy a truck yourself, and you finance it over 5 or 10 years, obviously if it doesn't go well, you're still on the hook for that debt, basically. You can try to sell the truck, obviously, but . . . [with MobiMunch] you have only a one-year commitment, so you can have a budget for the first year and give yourself a shock to see if you're going to make it or not. If you don't, you can hand the truck back to us at the end of that term. So it's a lower cost, lower risk as well, is the way I would describe it, because you have an end point in sight if it doesn't go well.

What is the process to rent a truck?

Most of the people who want to work with us will come and see the trucks in person so they kind of have a sense of what they're getting.

(continued)

(continued)

They come to the factory, they see how the trucks are made, they see similar trucks—it might not be the exact truck they're getting, but something similar, so they can get a sense of what it looks like. If they like the truck, the next step is typically a credit application. They go online and fill out a bunch of information about their bank history, their credit card history, that kind of stuff, to allow us to get a credit report and see whether they can pay their bills or not. Assuming that goes reasonably well—600-plus, let's call it—we would then gather all the information to produce a contract, and they would get a contract to sign, and they would sign the contract.

Q: What are the financial details? Is there a deposit, and what is the monthly fee—what does it start at?

So the deposit is typically anywhere between $5,000 and $15,000. There are two things that cause the deposit—obviously we have some deposit in all cases, in case there's damage to the truck. I would describe it as just like renting an apartment: you put down your security deposit, first/last month's rent, that kind of thing, in order to make sure that if there's damage to the apartment, the landowner has recourse or has capital ready to reinvest back into the property if you damage it. But also it's dependent on two main things: the creditworthiness of the applicant, so if the credit's not as good, you'd have a higher security deposit, and also the distance from Los Angeles. So in our particular case, that's a variable. Let's say you're in New York and you decide not to pay your bills and I have to repossess the truck. If I have to bring it all the way back here to Los Angeles to have it refurbished and send it out again, obviously that's a bit expensive, the shipping cost coast-to-coast. If you were in Orange County, just south of us in Los Angeles, obviously the shipping cost is a negligible thing if I need to repossess the truck, so basically that's a variable that affects our security deposit, in particular for our company.

Q: And then the monthly fee?

So that's just the security deposit; there are some other start-up expenses—the way I usually describe it is there are two categories. There's the start-up expenses and the ongoing expenses. The ongoing fees for the truck are anywhere from $3,000 to $4,000 per month.

That's the rental amount that you owe that depends on the size of the truck and whether the truck's newer or older or the design—there's a few variables that go into that. But obviously, an older design or older truck is going to be more in the $3,000 range, and a brand new truck is going to be more in that $3,750–$4,000 range. So that's where the disparity comes in the rental amount; it depends on the truck.

Q: Does the security deposit work the same way that it would with an apartment, where it's returned at the end of the contract?

Correct, less any money we've claimed to fix any damage to the truck.

Q: Now, if the operator wanted to make any enhancements or alterations, would that be a possibility? Who would handle that if so?

It's generally not recommended. If we do any enhancements at all, or changes, it would have to be done by us and our manufacturer, our manufacturing partner, which is AA Cater Truck here in Los Angeles, that's our manufacturing partner. If you made modifications to the truck when it was in your possession without discussing it with us first or having us do it, then the costs to remove those modifications would normally be taken out of your security deposit at the end of the contract. In terms of modifications, there are several problems with modifications. The first is that if we get that truck back after you don't want it for whatever reason, now we have to rent it to someone else, so we have a pretty standardized configuration. If you customize something to the point where it's really unique, then all the sudden it's very hard for us to rerent it, 'cause it's really designed for that one person's business. So if you really need something that unique, you're better off buying a truck and having it come from the manufacturer for you—it's a bigger capital expense, but if you really need something that customized, that's the way to do it. You buy it and you tailor it to pretty much whatever you want on a custom truck. If you want more fires or you want a burner instead of a griddle or whatever it is, you can do all that on a custom truck. The limitations—there are some, don't get me wrong—but with enough money, you can do just about anything you can do in a kitchen on a truck, basically. So that's one issue in terms of modifications.

(continued)

(continued)

Another is sometimes modifying a truck affects the health department process. So basically, if we have a truck that we know is NSF certified, AFC certified, and all the sudden now we change something on the truck, say we replace the grill with a char grill. Sounds pretty basic, oh, okay, we're just switching how we grill our food. Actually, that is the kind of thing that could affect whether you have to go through the whole process of getting it recertified with the health department and all that kind of stuff. So that's another issue: Do modifications have an impact on your health department permit?

The last piece is, and this is internally for us, our financing partner (for the same reasons we don't like to have nonstandardized trucks 'cause we may get it back and have to rerent it), well, they may get the truck back from us if we don't pay our bills and have to sell it or do something else with it, and they're not in the business of renting trucks. So basically, our financing partners sometimes don't let us modify a truck for the same reasons that we don't like to modify them ourselves in the sense of reusing it later for someone else or reselling it later to someone else.

Q: If there are any mechanical problems on the truck, who handles that?

Basically, it is not covered on a reconditioned vehicle, so a used vehicle we purchase and recondition typically has no warranty from the manufacturer and no warranty from us. If the truck is less than three years old and has less than 36,000 miles, very often there will be a manufacturer's warranty on the chassis and the drive train. If the truck is brand new, it would have to be a 36,000 mile on a Workhorse chassis, typically, and also a one-year parts warranty on the kitchen, so not a labor warranty, but parts on the kitchen. So I guess the question is if this is a new truck or a reconditioned truck. [Regarding coverage for repairs], if it's a reconditioned truck, then no; if it's a new truck then, yes, for a limited amount of time. But basically, on the reconditioned ones specifically, the operator pays for the maintenance as well as the repairs if there's a problem.

Picking a Commissary

When you operate on the road, it is important to have a clean, stable, and safe base of operations. A good commissary can make a huge difference in your ability to operate. The rules surrounding commissaries vary widely between different municipalities, so be sure to consult your local regulations and find a commissary that is compliant.

Depot versus Commissary

In New York City there is a legal distinction between a *depot*, where you are allowed to park a truck overnight, and a *commissary*, which is a depot where you are also allowed to prep food and store food overnight. This is important because ultimately you will need to find a nightly home for your truck as well as a facility to store all your food. Sometimes the two are not the same place. However, your life will be much easier if they are. If it is at all possible, you should attempt to keep your operations as simple as possible and have all your food storage and prep space close to where you are parking your truck at night.

Finding a Commissary

Depending on the infrastructure that already exists in your city, it might be very easy to find a commissary space. New York City and Los Angeles both have developed food truck markets and have a number of commissaries already in operation. However, smaller, developing food truck markets might not have commissaries in place. To find a commissary, the best place to start is by asking current vendors. If you cannot find a commissary you like, you can also try looking at private organizations with large cafeterias like office buildings, schools, churches, or culinary schools. Another good option is working out of a restaurant that only serves dinner. A restaurant that only serves dinner may not start doing prep until 11 AM. That works well for both the restaurant who can earn some revenue to offset their rent when their restaurant is idle and for a food truck that may want to do prep from 7 AM to 10 AM before lunch service.

Rent or Build?

In most cases you will want to rent commissary space. Depending on requirements and the options available in your town, you may want to consider building your own commissary. Building out a commissary space is bound to be an expensive proposition. Your commissary may cost more than your truck. Building regulations pertaining to the preparation of food are comprehensive, so be sure to review the regulations fully and get assistance from construction professionals who have built to local code in the past.

Work from Your Restaurant

If you already operate a restaurant, depending on your local laws, you might be able to use your restaurant space to support your trucks. Running mobile food operations out of an existing restaurant can strain relationships between truck staff and restaurant staff. It helps to have dedicated storage space in your restaurant to store inventory for the mobile food business. If your truckers come in before the restaurant opens and take the last of the salad, it will be very demoralizing for the restaurant workers. Also, if possible, make efforts to rotate staff between trucks and restaurants so that everyone can learn what is exciting and challenging about all parts of the business. This tends to improve communication and empathy across the organization.

Key Points of Consideration

When choosing a commissary, there are a number of criteria to consider including: price, service, accessibility to drive to your main vending locations, accessibility for you and your staff, whether there is covered outdoor space for your truck, distance between building and parking space, lot parking rules, parking lot security, the safety of the local neighborhood, consistent power to stay plugged in overnight (if you plan on keeping product refrigerated on the truck overnight), the overall cleanliness of the commissary, access to fresh water, ability to accept deliveries, access to ice, ability to dispose of dirty water, trash disposal, and ability to clean the truck. Visit several commissaries to get a feel for how each is run.

In addition to the basic services of parking spaces, power, water, and ice, some commissaries offer additional services to do purchasing on your behalf or do nightly cleaning of your trucks. Depending on your operation, this could be helpful.

Try to find a commissary where you have the same parking location every day and you are not "parked in" by other trucks. Once you spend $100,000 building a food truck, you don't want parking attendants moving your truck around at night. Invariably, there will be unexplained damage to the truck from bumping into other vehicles, and if the attendant forgets to plug in your shoreline after moving your truck, you could arrive the next morning to discover thousands of dollars' worth of ruined inventory.

Setting Up Your Space

Having a small private space on-site will help you coordinate the operations of your truck. If you have your own space or shared space in dry storage areas or walk-in coolers, be sure to organize it before your first day of operations. Figure out where product will be stored and the containers that you will use to store prepped vegetables or freshly baked cookies.

Your ability to manage your inventory will be a critical success factor. Trucks have limited storage space, and there can be big swings in sales depending on the weather and vending location. Nonetheless, you'll always want to have enough food and paper in stock, both on your truck and in your commissary to feed all your customers each day. If you run your inventory too low, you'll run out of items. If you run it too high, you risk food going bad. There is constant tension to figure out the correct inventory levels. It may take you a while to determine the correct inventory levels for your business.

As you set up an inventory system, you want to figure out the maximum amount of any item you'll need in inventory and the "par" or reordering point. The first thing you'll want to work toward is figuring out the rate at which you typically sell items. Initially this will be a theoretical number, and you will refine it as you operate. For example, if you sell 100 burgers on your truck with a 20% variance (so about 80 to 120 buns a day) and you only get deliveries Monday, Wednesday, and Friday, then you'll need to get three days' worth of buns in at a time. Three days' worth of buns is 360 buns. Just to be sure you don't run short, you might set the par a bit higher at 400. If you have 500 buns in inventory, you probably have more money invested in the buns than you need, and you also run the risk of the buns going bad. If you only have 100 buns and it is two days until your next delivery, you may run out.

Pars are helpful to manage ordering and to save enough space for your items. A best practice is to always keep your inventory in the same spot. If the spot is empty, it is a good reminder to reorder. If you move things around in the cooler or on your shelves, you may not notice you are out of milk because the cooler looks full.

Perishable items should always be rotated first in, first out (FIFO). This means that the oldest product you purchased should be used first. This prevents spoilage. Date perishable items when they are entered and physically rotate them on shelves so the oldest items are in the front and the newest are in the back.

Branding Fundamentals

From your business plan, you should have a logo and a rendering of the exterior of the truck. To build on those before your truck launches, you need to work out the aesthetics of a few more components of how the truck conveys its core messaging.

Exterior

The best advertising you'll have for your truck is the truck itself. When you design the exterior of the truck, think about how it is viewed from a distance and how it is seen up close. The exterior should be designed so it is visually digestible from a distance and up close. Food trucks are highly visible in the streetscape. Food trucks tend to be a single strong color so they are visible from a distance. Choose a color that pops. Think about the other iconic colors of food trucks in your city. Hopefully, the color you want isn't in use. Also, consider how your color will look if it gets a little dirty. Some paint colors hold up better with a little dirt than do others.

The truck design should also be interesting when viewed up close. Hopefully you will have dozens of customers patiently waiting in line for your amazing food. The truck design should be interesting and engaging up close. Obviously, they'll have your menu to look at, but it is good to give them visually interesting details as well as other ways to interact with the truck, perhaps via Twitter, Facebook, or Foursquare.

You can also include QR (Quick Response) codes to make it quick and easy for your customers to visit your website, like you on Facebook, and follow you on Twitter. These are the square bar codes that smartphones can read. All your customers have to do is snap a picture of the code on their phone. You can generate your QR Code for free online at sites like qrstuff.com, qrcode.kaywa.com, or delivr.com.

If you're planning on having any exterior lighting, be sure that you discuss it with your manufacturer ahead of time so that they can run power out to where it might be required. Exterior lights can make a truck a lot more visible if you plan to vend at night. Be sure to check local regulations to make sure your plans are permissible.

Packaging

Take the time to consider your packaging options. Packaging is an important differentiator. It has strong tactile, visual, and functional impacts on how your customers interact with your food. Once your customers leave your truck, all they will have to remember you by is the packaging and the food itself. Good packaging can reinforce your brand and improve the entire dining experience. Part of the reason customers pay a premium for Tiffany's products is the branded blue box. Tiffany's packaging is so much in demand that it has resale value on eBay. Be sure to try out your packaging with your products to make sure that they are functional. Does the soup container leak? Is it comfortable to eat from? If you can afford it, try to get packaging that is environmentally friendly. There are a number of great packaging options made from renewable materials like corn, potato, and sugar cane that are compostable. There are a number of purveyors who specialize in packaging that can help you find a good fit for your product. They can also preprint bags, cups, or cartons with your logo. Anything branded will need to be purchased ahead of time. One way to save some money during your opening is to buy branded stamps. Buy a big stamp for paper bags and a little stamp for cups.

Menu Board and Printed Menu

The menu is one of the major ways you communicate with customers. Not only does the menu need to clearly and effectively convey your menu offering, but it is an opportunity to convey your brand. Your menu should be visually compelling but clear. Make sure the font is large enough that your guests can see it from a distance. Think about how your eye moves through the menu and where it lingers. Think about the psychology of your pricing. How can you sell more sides or drinks? If you have any signature products, they should be given special emphasis. The menu should be designed to help your speed of service. If customers are constantly asking for clarification about particular aspects of your product, offering, you'll know you need to redesign the menu. You'll probably want to use a graphic designer to lay out your menu. You'll want a menu board for the truck, printed menus to hand out, especially if you want to promote delivery, and a catering menu. You'll probably need different versions of your menu, such as truck menu and catering menu, for the website as well. Many trucks use chalkboards or dry-erase boards for their menus. billyBoards (billyboardsmfg.com) specializes in chalkboards and sells a high-quality outdoor chalkboard. These types of menus are great because of their flexibility, especially if you run out of items. Just be sure to keep them clean! It may help to take a photo of the way you want the menu board to look every day. Then if it gets smudged, you'll be able to quickly change it back to the way you want it to look.

Music

Don't overlook the importance of music to the overall experience your customers will have when visiting your truck. You should curate music that is consistent with your brand. Create a playlist for an mp3 player or find an XM radio station that fits the tone you are looking for.

Website

Your Web presence will be an important part of the overall way in which customers interact with your brand. As you design your website, be sure that it reinforces your brand and has the most important information that customers will be looking for easily available. Key elements that should be incorporated into the website should be:

- Daily location and a schedule for the week
- Menu with pricing
- Links to Twitter and Facebook
- Newsletter sign-up
- Blog (if you plan to keep it updated)

For less than a hundred dollars, you can register a domain, set up a basic website on a standard content management platform like WordPress or Drupal. There are robust templates or themes for websites that are available for free or a small fee that you can customize for your business. However, because the experience customers have on the Web can dramatically influence their judgment about the professionalism of a brand, it might be worth investing more money to have a web developer build a site that is specific for your brand. From a technical perspective, you'll definitely want your site to be able to be viewed on phones or tablets. Mobile Meteor (mobilemeteor.com) has developed a great template for a mobile website specific to food trucks that is available for a few hundred dollars.

Blog

Blogging is time consuming, but it can be useful to help create connections with customers, and it keeps your website updated with new content, which is important for Google rankings. Something good to do while you're opening the truck is to write about the process on your website, but do not initially publish the blog posts. This will give you experience using the interface and a collection of content to draw upon when you need it, once you start operating the truck.

Professional Photography

Get your truck photographed when it is brand new and super clean. Wait for a sunny day and take it out to a couple of iconic places around town. Photograph it in a park with a bunch of friends hanging around it smiling. Photograph it with a long line of customers. Also, take photos of your food. Look at food magazines to see how similar food is styled for inspiration. You want your food to look beautiful and delicious. These photos will be great to have for your blog and to share on social media sites, but they will also be extremely helpful to have later on when you get media inquiries. Be sure to get high-res copies from your photographer so you can pass them along to journalists who end up writing about your truck. If you're looking to do this on a budget, you should stop by a local college with a photography program. Be sure to check the portfolios of the students you short-list to make sure you like their work.

Social Media

Social media has become an integral tool for many in the mobile food industry, and it will help to keep you connected with your customer and expand your customer base. If you haven't done so already, you should set up your business on Twitter, Facebook, and Foursquare. Get comfortable with the interfaces of each. Appendix C has a quick walk-through on how to set up an account in each of these social media sites.

Planning the Launch

At this point, one thing you're going to need to consider is how you want to launch the truck. Do you want to plan for a big splash on your opening day? Or do you want to have a soft opening so that you can work out your kinks slowly? There is no right answer to this. However, to any entrepreneurs who are running their first food business, I would recommend that you strongly consider full transparency from the start or a slow opening. Too many things can go wrong on day one that could create a lasting negative impression if there is too much hype built up about a truck and then it runs out of food on the first day or fails to operate correctly.

PR

Depending on your budget and the state and size of the local industry, it might make sense to hire a public relations firm for the launch of your business. PR companies that work in the food industry are experts at building media interest around new food ventures and can help you increase public awareness and interest in your business and the food that you serve, which can be especially important surrounding the launch or other key moments of growth or change. Some things to consider would be the company's relationships with food and small business media, previous experience, and reputation within the industry. PR companies charge on retainer or hourly basis, although emerging professionals in the field may consider working pro bono in order to expand their résumé and experience. You should feel comfortable in having a frank discussion about the amount of time you expect (and they plan) to invest in your project and in what are realistic goals and achievable results based on time and investment. Once you have hired your firm, you should also ask them to develop and share with you an announcement strategy, a story inventory, and list of media targets. They also can be helpful in helping you manage and leverage your social media platforms effectively.

Hiring

DEPENDING ON YOUR truck, you might be able to operate it on your own. However, if you need a team, be sure to hire very carefully. Before you start hiring, make sure your HR paperwork is in good shape so you can give your staff applications and professionally guide your new staff through required paperwork. As much as you are judging them through this process, they will be judging you.

Assembling a Team

Every market is a little bit different. However, based on talking with entrepreneurs in several cities, it seems that, generally, the best candidates come from referrals and Craigslist. Talk to other entrepreneurs in the restaurant industry and in the food truck business to see where they find staff.

Use your job descriptions to write your job post. And once you've written the job post, save it somewhere so you can use it again and again. Be sure to give as much information about what you are looking for as possible. If you know the times the shifts will run, put them in the ad.

Be bluntly honest about what is required from your staff. They should know that it isn't just about having fun and waving out the window of the truck. There will be fast and furious lunch rushes and a lot of cleaning. Be open about what is great about the job and what is hard. Yes, in the spring and fall there isn't a better job than to be out on the streets in amazing weather. However, in winter it is very cold, and in the summer it is very hot.

Hard Skills

Almost everything that needs to be done on a food truck can be taught, so long as your team has the desire and drive to learn. However, there are a few hard things you may want to screen for, including driving and availability. If you need staff that can drive (and are willing to drive), be sure to make it part of the ad. Look for staff that can commit to working the whole season. If you work year-round, warn them that winter is cold on the truck and the summer is very, very hot, but you are looking for people to stay. If you are looking for staff just for the summer, let them know. Structure employment bonuses to incentivize your employees to stay for the entire season. (After the first year, you'll see how these have worked out, and you can adjust these to make them work better.)

Soft Skills

Energy: Do they smile easily? Do they glow? Is energy apparent in their résumés and cover letters?

Integrity: Do they look you in the eye? Do they have a good hand-shake? Are they honest about their past experiences? Will they do a thorough job and take pride in their work?

Intelligence: Are they curious about how their role fits into the larger role of the restaurant? Do they want to learn about all aspects of the operation? Do they ask insightful questions?

Maturity: Have they had responsibility in past jobs? Will they treat employees and customers with respect?

Example Questions

Here are some questions to help you with interviewing.

1. Why did you leave your last job? How did you leave your last job?
2. What did you like (and dislike) about your last job?
3. Tell me about a recent memorable meal or food experience.
4. Why do you want to work in food?
5. What makes a good food trucker?

6. Tell me about a time when you dealt with a customer well. Why do you think you dealt well with him or her?
7. Tell me about a time when you dealt with a customer poorly, and why you think you dealt poorly with him or her?

Avoid asking hypothetical questions because people can say anything in an interview. Probe for actual experiences about what they did and how they think about it now. As you interview more people, you'll develop questions that help you discern who is a strong candidate for the job.

Check References

No matter how busy you are, always check references for your shortlisted candidates. Most savvy applicants know the right answers to give in an interview to sound good. You need to discern if they are as good as they sound. The best way to do that is to speak with people who have worked with them in the past. Important questions to ask of a former employer are:

1. Would you hire them back?
2. How did you manage them to get the best work out of them?
3. What were their strengths and weaknesses?

Because many of your applicants will have worked in hospitality, checking references is also a good way to potentially network. Get to know the other hospitality professionals in your town.

Initial Training

Do your best to schedule trainings with the entire group at once. Cross-train everyone at everything. Training the group all at once will save you time and also help build cohesiveness across the team. Ultimately, because it helped start the business, the opening team will have a special bond and will tend to last longer and be more vested in your business than future employees.

Picking Vending Locations

WHETHER YOU ARE doing street vending or picking a lot, getting the right location is paramount.

Researching Vending Locations

The three most important things to keep in mind regarding picking vending spots for your truck are location, location, location. Something as small as being on the wrong side of the street, picking a spot in the shade versus in the sun (or vice versa), or being in the middle of the block instead of on the corner can have a big effect on sales.

As you research places to vend, you should consider placement and visibility. Is there enough room for your truck? Does it fit into the streetscape? Is your truck visible from the typical direction potential customers might approach? Also, be on the lookout for "feeders" to bring out foot traffic. Traditional feeders include: movie theaters, event spaces, shopping corridors, and subway stations.

I recommend scouting for location on foot or by bike. When you go by car, it is too easy to overlook the subtleties of how people are moving through the space. And most important, you aren't able to interact with permanent members of the community to learn more about the habits and preferences of the people in that neighborhood. Also, be sure to find a convenient, publically accessible restroom for your staff, or negotiate access to a private one. Locate the nearest ATM if you don't take credit cards so you can direct customers there who are short on cash. Finally, note the nearest bank in case you need to get change during service.

Even when you are passing through a neighborhood quickly, take the time to talk to people who will have an eye on the street. Doormen, building managers, and security guards will know a lot about the nature of the street and how people in the neighborhood behave.

If you are vending in a market that allows trucks to move to different spaces over time, you should keep a journal of potential locations. A sample location sheet is included in Appendix A. You never know when an errand might bring you to a new part of town that will have a spot that could end up being perfect for street vending.

Living the Spot

Once you have a short list of potential locations, you should do your best to get out and "live" the location. Always visit the locations you are planning to vend multiple times. Watch the location at different times of the day to see who is out, what traffic is like, and where people are going.

At the very least, you will need to visit two specific times: at your arrival time and during your peak vending time. It is always good to arrive during the morning to see what the parking situation is like around the time your truck would ordinarily arrive. If parking is very hard, you may need to start your day earlier to get a spot at this location, or it might be so hard to park it isn't worth trying. It is also important to visit the location during the meal period at the time you want to vend to watch traffic patterns on the street.

When you are "living" the spot, you will want to make a map of the location that has some key information on it, including:

- What other storefronts are selling
- Names of contacts at local businesses
- Other street vendors
- The nearest bank (to get change)
- The nearest public restroom
- Parking rules on the streets
- A prioritized list of the best parking locations (1, 2, 3, . . . , etc.)

First Day!

Once you've done your research, you're ready to try out your new location. Whenever you are trying a location for the first time, you should always give yourself a bit of extra time to park. Also, you should always have a backup in case something unexpected happens on your first day.

Getting parked at your preferred location is obviously of the utmost importance. Here are a few tricks to help you get the spot you want:

- **Stick and hold!** Many parking spots are held by people running errands or doing deliveries; often if you are patient, the spot you want will open up.
- **Check meters!** Look at the meters to see if one is expiring soon.
- **Trade locations:** If you have a spot that isn't ideal, keep an eye on the spot you want. Many drivers will trade spots if you need the help.
- **Call the owner of a commercial vehicle:** Most commercial vehicles will have a number on the door. If you call the owner and tell them the plates on the vehicle, they might be able to page the driver and get them to swap with you. Be super friendly and gracious if they are willing to help!

Once you are parked, you should immediately get out and pick up the area around your truck. Pick up any trash, even if it isn't yours. Then, as your preparation allows, make the rounds and introduce yourself to everyone you met while doing your research. Say hi to the building managers and security guards and invite them over for lunch. If there are vendors who don't want you there, you should be sure to make eye contact when you say hello to them.

The biggest mistake you can make on your first day is showing up at a new location without doing your research.

Interview 4: Kim Ima of The Treats Truck on Choosing Vending Locations

The Treats Truck opened in New York City in 2007 and was one of the first branded, gourmet trucks in the city. Kim still works the truck almost every day. Kim is observant and completely engaged with everyone who comes to the truck. Odds are that she can guess the cookie that you didn't even know you wanted.

Q: What are your best spots usually like? What makes a spot bad?

It's totally random! Midtown spots were awesome, but then the zoning changed. Spots near subways and offices are usually good. I park in neighborhoods sometimes. Good spots aren't always the flashy ones. It has to do with the vibe of the street, whether there's a lot of foot traffic, and if the foot traffic is leisurely. If everyone walking on the street is "in the zone" and the block is just a passageway, it's not a good spot because no one will stop to buy anything. You have to check each spot against three factors: the health department rules, the street signs (which are often ambiguous), and the reality of the street.

Q: How do you troubleshoot parking?

Trial and error. You just have to go out there with your list of possibilities and scout it out. I found my best spot—38th and 5th—completely by accident. We were scouting parking, and we were so frustrated and overwhelmed that I just decided to pull over for a moment and think. And then people started coming up to the window and asking, "What do you have in there?" You just have to get to know the city. Do your research and walk around. And don't assume that your first day or first few weeks is a representative sample . . . good spots change seasonally, so you have to keep scouting for new spots all the time.

Q: How often do you park in the same spots?

We park in two spots each day, and I try to keep the location consistent on a weekly basis. This means I get different regulars in different spots.

Q: What is the parking etiquette for your truck? Do you have arrangements with other trucks about spots and when you'll be there?

I try to use common sense and courtesy, respect, and awareness. I don't park right next to a truck or business selling baked goods. It's pretty obvious when there's another vendor nearby who isn't happy because often their employees will just come and stand nearby with their arms crossed and stare you down. I build rapport with other vendors by

(continued)

(continued)
giving them free cookies. Know when you're the new guy and be willing to learn. Be open.

Q: What is the best way to interact with other food trucks? How do you handle arguments over parking and the like?

Courtesy, respect, and free cookies.

Q: How often does your truck get ticketed?

About three or four times per year.

Q: What's the largest fine your truck has ever received?

Average fine is $65; highest fine was $115.

Q: Do you try to contest tickets most times, or do you just pay them?

Most of the time I just pay them. A few times I've contested, like when traffic prevented me from getting through an intersection or when I had paid for parking but the meter people didn't see the receipt on my dash. But in general, it takes a long time to contest them, so I just pay them because my time is already stretched so thin.

The Opening Schedule

In ORDER TO stay organized as you work toward opening your truck, I'd highly recommend using an opening checklist. An opening checklist presumes you have already developed your concept, your brand, chosen your truck, and have your core management team in place.

Spreadsheet software such as Microsoft Word, Google Docs, or Apple Numbers are well suited to tracking the information you'll want to capture in an opening countdown. Ideally you'll have columns to track: weeks until opening, task category, task, responsible parties (or "owners" of the task), dependencies, and the date the task was completed. A sample opening checklist is included in Appendix A.

If you plan on eventually running multiple trucks, you might want to consider investing in rudimentary project management software to track dependencies and measure the actual time it took to complete parts of the project against your projections. This will help you get better and better at truck openings.

Timing

Timing your opening is of crucial importance. Ideally, you want to open a month or so before the prime selling season starts. When you initially open your truck, many of the aspects of the operations that you so meticulously planned for won't work out as you anticipated. You should give yourself at least two weeks of troubleshooting before you can expect the truck to be operating at a high level of efficiency.

Also, delays that you never anticipated will happen. So budgeting some flex time into your schedule will be prudent. Kitchen equipment might arrive damaged and prevent you from getting your truck built out in time for your scheduled inspection, for instance.

Key Categories

Administrative

- Set up business as legal entity
- Credit sheet established, vendor credit established
- Register truck
- Set up liability insurance, auto insurance
- Set up unemployment account
- Set up new payroll account
- Choose register or POS
- Purchase register or POS
- Set up register or POS

Food and Beverage

- Finalize menu
- Finalize recipes
- Finalize kitchen equipment
- Calculate theoretical food costs
- Set up ordering system and pars
- Set up storage
- Place initial orders and receive food

Commissary

- Choose commissary location
- Waste removal procedures reviewed and carting finalized
- Hire prep staff if required
- All pars established and inventory storage system
- Train food prep staff
- Begin receiving nonperishable food items
- Set up storerooms/metroshelves
- Big cleaning and setup of commissary space

Truck Construction

- Purchase or rent a truck
- Choose a fabricator
- Draft kitchen layout

- Test kitchen layout
- Truck construction complete

Kitchen Equipment

- Finalize kitchen equipment
- Order kitchen equipment
- Kitchen equipment received and warranties filed
- Turn on and test all equipment
- Train opening team on equipment operation and troubleshooting

HR

- Set up system to file employee paperwork
- Develop theoretical staffing schedule to determine number of staff to hire
- Place ad locally for staff needs
- Begin interview process
- Hire
- Finalize preopening training schedule dates
- Distribute schedule to staff: seven-day count
- Whole-staff orientation day (all staff finish paperwork)

Licensing

- Apply for all required licenses and permits
- Receipts and posting of all permits
- Health inspection scheduled

Printer

- Design menus, business cards, T-shirts, uniforms, etc.
- Finalize and order take-out menus and business cards
- Receive take-out menus and business cards

Office

- Set up office space
- Order and schedule safe install
- Tailor unit specific documents

- Delivery of safe
- Submit information for first payroll
- Organize all electronic documents on cloud-based storage like Google Docs, Dropbox, or Egnyte so they can be shared with managers
- Set up printer and fax
- Employee telephone list (cell phones, etc.)
- Key box with master keys

PR/Marketing

- Set up social media accounts for Facebook, Twitter, Foursquare, etc.
- Finalize and submit all hours of operation
- Website update: hours, location, phone number, map, etc.
- Decide opening schedule
- Schedule photo shoot for truck
- Reach out to local press and food blogs about opening

Signage

- Truck exterior design
- Design exterior menu and press display
- Menu board sized and frame sized and ordered
- Legal and health signs ordered
- Attain health department signage: decide on posting locales
- Get truck painted or wrapped
- In-store posters and promotional signage delivered
- Sign day: install all signs, water, bathroom, CPR, etc.
- Install exterior menu and press display

Smallwares

- Linens contract finalized
- Schedule first linen delivery
- Edit smallwares opening inventory
- Smallwares bid, priced, and ordered
- Receive smallwares
- First linen delivery
- Set in place clean smallwares
- Place opening paper products order
- Receive paper

Succeed: Doing One Truck Right

THIS SECTION OF the book focuses on getting your truck operating smoothly and profitably. As in any business, it is often advantageous to get the simplest component of the business up and running successfully before looking to grow. The following chapter includes a number of tips and suggestions for success in the daily operation of your truck.

Responsible Vending

Food trucks suffer from a lot of bad stereotypes. It is up to the entire vending community to work harder to improve the standing of food truck vendors in the public's imagination. Be nice to everyone you meet. It is essential to be a good neighbor and an active participant in the communities in which you are vending.

Respecting the Local Community

Street vending is a privilege, not a right. It is up to the truck owners to be mindful of the needs of the community in which they vend. First and foremost, park responsibly. Don't compromise public safety by blocking crosswalks or fire hydrants. Next, be clean. Run your operation to the highest standards of food safety. Not only should you run your own operation cleanly, but you should make sure that you leave the local neighborhood cleaner than you found it. Every day when you arrive, clean the street around your truck, and before you leave, sweep up around your truck again. If there are public trash cans, make sure your customers didn't drop anything on the ground nearby. Never dump wastewater or oil on the street or down a sewer drain. Protect the environment as best as you can. Use high-efficiency, soundproofed generators. Use recycled or green paper products whenever possible. Never idle your engine for more than three minutes. The best way to earn the respect of local communities is by giving back. Participate in fundraisers for local schools, hospitals, fire departments, and police departments. Help revitalize public spaces. As you do good work, you will slowly be accepted and incorporated into the local community.

Respect Other Mobile Vendors

While you might be attracted to the idea of street vending because of the promise of independence, it is important to realize you are a part of the larger community of street vendors and that your actions can impact the well-being of other vendors. Take the time to get to know the other vendors in your city. While you are competitors, you are also collaborators. There is definitely work that can be done that can increase the pie for all street vendors. A great example is food truck festivals, food truck lots, or food truck pods. When trucks with complementary products vend together, it tends to stimulate demand, and they all do better.

It is poor form to "roll up" on other vendors' established spots without calling ahead. If you are going to a location where other people are already vending, even if it is on a day when that vendor isn't ordinarily there, give them a call. This is a great opportunity to network and to learn about the neighborhood. Most vendors will appreciate hearing from you and will share details about the neighborhood to help you succeed. They can tell you who is friendly toward trucks and who isn't. If you get to a vending location and someone is there whom you didn't expect, talk to them. If they tell you the block is too "hot" to support more business, please respect that and try somewhere else. This isn't necessarily about avoiding competition, rather, it is about not "overfishing" the location. Some locations can support a lot of trucks, but some places can support a lot less. The vendors on the street today spent months with paltry yields to build some of these locations up to be the food truck hubs they are today. Give the guys who have been around some credit, and then take some of your own by finding a new spot and sharing it.

Respect the Law

A food truck is a viable hospitality business. Because of the low capital to start a food truck and the low overhead, the economics of food trucks are relatively forgiving. Food trucks don't require dodging the law to turn a profit. Not paying taxes might seem like a good strategy, but it is shortsighted on two accounts: First, if you're caught, the consequences are dire, and second, underreporting your sales or paying employees off the books holds back the entire industry by making it seem less financially important than it is. Correctly record your sales. Pay the state the sales tax you collected. Pay your employees on the books. Pay income tax. Pay any parking fines or violations promptly. Operating your business legitimately provides your municipality with the resources it needs to pay for a number of activities that improve the business environment for food trucks, such as maintaining roads and funding economic development.

Do Well by Doing Good

If food trucks behave responsibly, more and more communities will be won over by the many positive benefits that food trucks generate. Food trucks provide diverse, interesting, culinary offerings. They bring energy and excitement to the streets and drive foot traffic to neighborhoods. Food trucks watch the streets and help keep them safe and clean.

Vending Locations

WHILE TRUCKS OFFER the promise of mobility and flexibility, in reality, most trucks habitually stick to the same locations over time. Many trucks are in the same location day after day. Other trucks rotate spots daily but are in the same location on the same day each week.

To some extent, the type of food you are selling will dictate how you park. The more accessible your food, the greater ability you'll have to stay put during the week. If you sell sandwiches, salads, pizza, or burgers, you can be at the same office park all week long, and your fans might come two or three times a week while you're there. The more exotic your food, the more you'll have to move. While your fans might love your delicious kati rolls, most Americans will want Indian food only about once a week. You'll probably be better served by frequenting five different locations throughout the week and having customers "wait" for Indian day!

Take a couple of hours off the truck once a week to wander around and explore new locations. It takes a long time to find and build a good vending location. You might need to invest weeks or months in building spots to attract regulars. This takes time and effort, but in the long term, it is the best way to go. Once you find and build a new spot, you can trade with the other trucks: "Oh, this new spot is great. I go on Tuesday through Thursday. You should check it out on Wednesday." Don't give up on a new location in one day.

Improved Street Vending Locations

If your sales are slow, mix up your vending locations. Try putting your truck near parks, office parks, mass transit hubs, landmarks, museums, shopping destinations, street level malls, beaches, college campuses, and central business districts. Try different times of day, such as testing out a breakfast item with coffee in the morning or partnering with a bar or a nightclub in the evening.

Catering Private Events

In addition to street vending, look into catering special events. Catering events are great business because they are guaranteed revenue. Even if it rains, you'll know you'll be able to make a sale. Potential catering clients include film shoots, corporate events, bar mitzvahs, birthday parties, and weddings.

When you price your catering menu, you should structure it with a location fee and a minimum for food as well as an hourly fee. The location fee should change depending on the location. If you need to travel a long way to cater the event, you should raise the fee. The location fee should include the first two to three hours of service. The minimum ensures that you're making enough off of the event to be sure you make more than you might if you were out vending a normal shift. If you make more money at lunch than dinner, your minimum should be higher at lunch than dinner. Finally, the hourly fee is to cover the cost of your labor if you get booked for a longer event. There is a big difference between serving 100 people at a wedding depending on whether you are at the venue to provide snacks from 4 PM to 10 PM or if you are just serving a late night snack to guests from 9 PM to 10 PM. It is the same amount of food, but in one case you're tied up for six hours and in the other for only one hour.

Vending at Special Events

Special events can be amazing opportunities to vend. Food truck vending events, flea markets, car shows, night markets, beer tastings, and concerts are all great places to show up with a food truck. Often special events are structured either as a percentage rent, a fixed fee, or some combination of the two. Generally a percentage rent of around 10 percent maxes out what food trucks can reasonably do and still expect to make a profit. If you agree to do an event at a certain percentage of the revenue, be accurate when paying. You may think that you're making money by underreporting, but you're just making it harder for the promoter to make their ends meet. The promoter will be judging your success at the event by the fee you paid. If you didn't offer much in fees, they may assume you didn't do well and replace you with another vendor in their next event. It really pays in the long term to be honest and forthright about your sales.

Any group of food trucks vending together will stimulate demand. Take the initiative to organize your own events. A group of trucks will be able to have wider appeal because of the variety of food they can offer as well as the fact that they can combine marketing efforts. For example, the 30 members of the New York City Food Truck Association have more than 250,000 Twitter followers as a group. As a group, your voice and ability to promote yourself improve. Plus, when customers come to food truck events, they come to eat. So sales can be even better at a food truck event than at a music festival, where the customers are coming primarily to listen to music. Once you start doing events, you'll get a sense of what events will be moneymakers. A good rule of thumb to get you started is at least 750 attendees per truck for an event where people are coming to eat or 1,500 attendees per truck for an event where people are coming to do something else like listen to music or shop at an outdoor market.

Interview 5: Jen Lyon of MeanRed Productions on Food Truck Events

MeanRed (meanredproductions.com) has built a reputation for multigenre events, often staged in quirky venues and spaces, and which always feature great music. The last Parked! at South Street Seaport attracted 25,000-plus attendees.

Q: What makes a successful food truck event?

A successful Parked! is full of moving parts—it's not just a food truck bonanza. There are cooking lessons for kids and a plethora of distractions for while you're waiting in line—like magicians, for instance. The stage of great bands is visible from every perspective. We're originally known for our music curation, so you can always expect really talented acts on our stage. We try to book bands that can be enjoyed by all! And, of course, a well-stocked beer garden and lots and lots of food trucks!

Our first *Parked!* event was staged at BKLYN Yard, a little outdoor lot on the Gowanus Canal. That first year, we had only a handful of trucks, and some of our confirmed vendors didn't even show up. That was a challenge. We realized that in order to be successful in the future, we needed to win over the trust of the food truck owners. Our attitude became, "We're all in it together." Just as they are small businesses taking a risk on their overall expenses to participate in a *Parked!* event, we're taking a risk as well on the full event production costs. We respect each truck operator as a small business—just like us—by always keeping the bottom line in sight. Last year, over 35 food trucks came to South Street Seaport.

Q: What are some of the problems you've run into while working with food trucks?

The production logistics can become exceedingly complicated. Just getting the trucks into the lot can be difficult. If the turnout isn't as expected, we're all disappointed and vow to try again harder next time!

Q: What is the right ratio between number of customers and trucks?

You need to have at least one truck for every 850 guests or so for a five- to eight-hour event.

Q: What do you look for in a potential venue?

Primarily, we look for a venue owner who is invested in the mission of presenting engaging and diverse cultural programming and for someone who has lots of patience and can handle the difficult logistics of loading in so many trucks.

Q: Do you prefer ticketed events or pay-as-you-go events?

We produce both kinds of events for different reasons. *Parked!* typically is free, whereas our Oktoberfest is ticketed. We love being able to present as many pay-as-you-go events as possible because it puts the power to decide in the hands of the people. Often, however, ticketing is important for crowd control and to create a smaller, more dynamic event!

(continued)

(*continued*)

Q: What would you recommend to someone organizing their first food truck event?

Build a strong relationship with your vendors, and think of other festival activities so everyone has entertainment all day.

Q: How can readers get in touch with you if they want to hire you to help them organize an event?

Hit us up directly! Info@meanredproductions.com.

Learn from Customers

Ask your customers for advice. Many trucks have a great dialogue with their customers via Twitter, Facebook, and, of course, face-to-face when they are vending on the street.

Watch your customers' behavior, and adjust your operations accordingly. Early in the book, I told you that faster is better. In general, this is true. The one exception to this rule is when you have no line. Sometimes having a bit of a line around your truck can be helpful as it demonstrates that your truck is interesting and popular. Consumers tend to stop and investigate if a truck seems to be busy.

Building Spots

Building up a new location takes time. While social media lets you announce a new location to customers you have, many of your current customers may not be close enough to take advantage of the new locations you find, so you will be slowly finding and building new regulars over time at each new location where you vend.

The best thing you can do to help build a following in a new location is to go to that location consistently week after week on the same day. Encourage the customers who find you to come back next week at the same time and to bring their friends. Slowly, your fan base in the neighborhood will grow.

Another way to get a foothold in a new neighborhood is to reach out to local businesses. Office workers are often avid food truck customers.

You can learn the names of the local businesses in your neighborhood by visiting office buildings and looking at the tenants, by asking building managers or security guards, or by asking your regulars. Google Maps also offers a feature where if you zoom in closely enough, you can see the names of local businesses. With the list of local businesses in hand, you can reach out to the Twitter feeds for those businesses or try to get in touch with an office manager. Many times companies appreciate learning about new food options that are nearby and will feature your business in internal newsletters.

Managing the Team

THERE ARE A few concepts out there that could be run as a solo operation. Many trucks start with family or friends pitching in to get things going, but at some point most trucks will require a team of some sort to operate. The hospitality industry is notorious for turnover, so bringing in and retaining great people will be an important aspect of building a business that can last.

While you might want to do everything yourself when you start, in time you're going to want to be able to take a break to spend evenings or weekends with your family or to take a week off to go on holiday.

Hiring Right

The best thing you can do to improve the quality of your team is to hire better people. Invest the time to hire great people. It is really worth taking the time to find great candidates. Also, do what you can to pay a competitive wage. Higher wages tend to get you more responsible employees.

Building a Culture

Everyone wants to feel that they are part of something. Build a culture of responsibility and caring around your truck. Developing a culture is a great way to build bonds with your staff and between your staff. If there is a shared purpose, your team will be more cohesive and cooperative and more committed.

Incentives

In general, because there is a lot more responsibility associated with running a truck, you're going to need to pay a bit more than brick-and-mortar restaurants to bring in the talent you need. Use bonuses to retain staff for the season. However, it is even more fun and rewarding for the team to get surprise bonuses when things go well. If you have a really great day, do something nice for the team. Treat them to dinner or buy them something special you know they'll like.

Training

Take the time to bring new hires up to speed on your operations. Just throwing new hires in to "sink or swim" is a recipe for disaster. Don't just teach your employees *how* to do their job but also *why* you want them to do it a specific way. "Why" is the most important aspect of training. If your employees don't understand the reason you want things done a certain way, they will take shortcuts that might compromise the intent of what you would like them to accomplish.

Ensure that everyone knows your menu and ingredients by heart. A great tool to help with this is a list of menu descriptions. Everyone who interacts with customers should be able to speak eloquently about the food. Everyone should know the ingredients and common allergens that are present in different recipes, such as milk, soy, wheat, and nuts.

Remember driving school! Driving a food truck is a bit more complicated than driving a car. Even if your employees have licenses, they should go to driving school with you or a preapproved driver to demonstrate that they can safely drive the vehicle. The food truck is the entire business. If it gets into an accident, everyone on your team will be out of work. It is important to drive conservatively.

Note: Moving violations should be the responsibility of the employee. As a food truck owner, your interests are aligned with the local police when it comes to speeding, reckless driving, driving without a seatbelt, or any other behavior that puts the vehicle, its occupants, or others at risk.

Also, if you don't train, things will get done over time but maybe not the way you want them done. Employee training must be ongoing:

- Product knowledge quizzes
- Tasting of all menu items
- Communications training
- Service tests
- Point of sale (POS) drills
- Personal hygiene training and checks

Being the Boss

A few good rules for new managers are the following:

- **Lead by example:** Don't just tell your employees what to do. Show them how to do it. Rather than say, "Go take out the trash," grab a trash bag and say, "Will you help me take out the trash?"
- **Listen:** Many managers make the mistake of talking too much and listening too little. Unless you know where they are coming from, it will be hard to persuade your employees to change their behavior. Also, your employees may know more about some aspect of your operation than you do; for instance, if they've come from another truck or another restaurant, they might have ideas about how things should work that are even better than what you've come up with so far.
- **Don't abuse your power:** If you're rude and disrespectful to your team, they will be rude and disrespectful to your guests. A culture of caring and hospitality starts at the top.

  If you're new to being in charge, you should take a look at an excellent article from the *Harvard Business Review* called, "Becoming the Boss" by Linda A. Hill. While it is written for a corporate audience, the common mistakes of new food truck managers are the same.[18]

  If you don't have a copy yet, order *Setting the Table* by Danny Meyer today. It is a great read about building up a culture that cares about service and hospitality.

Put It on Paper

You MAY HAVE the entire operation worked out in your head, but it is essential that you get that information put on paper so it can be shared with your team. Checklists are one of the most important things you implement to avoid mistakes.

Resources

- Credit sheet
- Important numbers
- Staff list
- Schedule template
- Truck binder
    - Legal information
    - Health information

HR Forms

- Application
- New hire packet
- Policy manual
- One-pager

Operational Forms

- Daily sales sheet
- Daily log
- Drawer count

- Safe count
- Order sheet

Training Materials

- Daily checklists
- Weekly checklists
- Monthly checklists
- Job descriptions
- Recipes
- Line manual
- Menu descriptions

Regularly Update

Once every six months, you should review all your materials to make sure they reflect the reality of what your daily operations are like.

Watching the Numbers

BUDGETING IS THE single most important thing you can do to improve the performance of your business. An oft-quoted aphorism in business is that to manage something, you need to measure it. However, just as important as the measurement is the comparison of that measurement against some sort of benchmark. Fortunately, since you took the time and care to develop a business plan, you have a head start for your first year of a budget to track your progress against.

Measure to Manage

You will generate a lot of useful data as you operate your truck. This data will be extremely helpful as your business develops and grows. One of the most important things you can do from the start is to track your sales by location and weather. Before you go out on your first day of sales, you should set up a spreadsheet with the following columns: Day of the Week, Date, Shift (Bfst/Lunch/Dinner/Late Night), Sales, Temp., Precip., and Notes.

Within a few months, you will have learned exactly where your best locations are and what sorts of sales you can expect based on the weather. This will help you set pars so you know how much food to send out on your truck and so you can balance the competing needs of not running out of food while simultaneously not wasting food.

After a year, you will have detailed knowledge about the seasonality of your business. You will know the amount of precipitation at which customers will be reluctant to come out.

Daily Break-Even Analysis and Daily Revenue Goals

You should know the number of sales you need to make each day to breakeven for a typical shift. Your first hurdle in running a food truck is not to lose money running a shift. Every shift has expenses associated with it: the labor required to get the truck prepped and on location, the food that will be prepared that will go bad if it isn't sold, and the fuel used to be on the street. Knowing the bare minimum you need to make to breakeven will help you make decisions about whether to operate or not on very cold, very hot, or rainy days.

The equation for your revenue breakeven is as follows:

$$\text{Revenue (Breakeven to Be Profitable)} = (\text{Labor} + \text{Costs/Shift} + \text{Fixed Costs})/\text{COGS}$$

Now that you have written a business plan and perhaps started your operations, you'll have a much clearer idea of the costs associated with running a shift.

Goals are important because they help motivate staff and highlight potential changes that might need to be made operationally to achieve them. It goes without saying that your goal should be higher than your breakeven. The daily goal should incorporate your knowledge about the location where you are vending for the day, the weather, and any other relevant factors including whether it is a holiday or whether you are running a promotion that might influence sales.

If your daily breakeven is $500, you might set a goal of $800 for a relatively good location on a moderate day. If it is a great location, the goal might be $1,000. If it is a great location on a cold day with a 15 percent chance of rain in the forecast, you might give yourself a goal of $550.

Keep track of your sales daily, the goals you give yourself, and whether you hit them. As time goes on, you will get better and better at anticipating the sales.

There are certain circumstances in which it might be worth running a shift even if it isn't profitable. This is because certain fixed costs like the commissary rent and insurance are "sunk costs," meaning that they have already been paid, or are committed to pay, so they aren't relevant to your decision. You don't need to make enough revenue to pay for the rent for the day to make it worth running the truck. If you can make just $1 toward the rent, economically it is worth running the shift. To determine the point at which your operations start contributing to fixed costs, use this calculation:

$$\text{Revenue (Breakeven to Contribute to Fixed costs)} = \text{(Labor + Costs/Shift)/COGS}$$

If your revenue to breakeven is $500/shift, your revenue to start contributing to the fixed costs might only be $350/shift. If you think you can make $400 on a rainy day, economically you should go out because it will help pay for some of the fixed costs like rent. However, the short-term economic viability is just one of many factors to consider when cutting a shift. Two other very important criteria are customer expectations (will you be letting down hard-core regulars?) and staff expectations (will they be sad they lost hours or happy not to work a slow day when they wouldn't earn tips anyway?).

If you find that a certain day of the week is consistently slow, you might want to take a break that day. This is a good opportunity to rest the team and get maintenance done on the truck. Typically, Mondays are the slowest day of the week for street vending, so if you want to take a day off, Monday is a good day to start.

Weekly Profit and Loss Check

A good rule of thumb to follow is to review the two major costs of your truck on a weekly basis: COGS and labor. You can quickly get an estimate of your COGS by summing all of your food and paper purchases for the week. If you are doing weekly inventory, you can get a more exact number by starting with the value of your opening inventory, adding your purchases, and then subtracting your ending inventory.

$$\text{COGS} = \text{Opening Inventory} + \text{Purchases} - \text{Ending Inventory}$$

$$\text{COGS/Weekly Revenue} = \text{COGS}\%$$

And you can quickly get your labor costs by summing your payroll for the week. The easiest way to get this might be to get your total payroll for the week from your payroll service provider, but you can also estimate it quickly by summing the product of the hours each employee worked times their wages and multiplying the result by the payroll taxes that apply in your municipality. If you don't know the payroll taxes that will be applied, you can get an estimate from your payroll provider or your accountant. A good estimate might be 11 or 12 percent.

Labor = Sum of (Hours × Wages) for Each Employee × 1.12

By tracking your major costs weekly, you can have a good degree of confidence that your numbers will track well on a monthly basis.

Monthly Review of Books

Accounting may seem like a waste of time that is a distraction from your "real" business, but doing the books will give you the information you need to effectively manage your business. On a monthly basis, you should look over the books and see where your money is going. You should ask yourself if it feels right. This is a great opportunity to remind yourself where your money is going and reflect on how you might run your business more efficiently. If you see any costs start to move up as a percentage of revenue, you need to move quickly to keep them in check. Pennies grow into dollars very quickly in this business.

Manage Costs to Your Budget

If at some point, on a daily, weekly, or monthly basis, it becomes apparent that your revenues aren't what you thought they might be or that your costs are higher than you anticipated, you need to act quickly to bring your costs in line with your revenue. You need to watch the numbers to manage your business. However, watching the numbers alone doesn't help. You need to find the reasons why they are changing. That may mean digging into point of sales reports or flipping through lots of old invoices. Watching the details closely will give you the information you need to run your business efficiently.

Purchasing

Based on your sales, you should know the five items you buy most frequently. If you sell burgers and hand-cut fries, you probably buy a lot of ground beef and potatoes. For the items you spend the most money on, you should be checking your prices on every invoice. If there are fluctuations, you should contact your vendors immediately. For the rest of the items on your order sheet, sit down once a month and check your order sheet against recent invoices to see in which direction your prices are going.

If prices are increasing dramatically, you might need to consider changing menu items, looking for substitutes, or raising prices. Constantly keep on the lookout for new vendors that offer competitive pricing on the goods and services you use. A good rule of thumb is to get at least three quotes for any substantial purchase.

Refining the Menu

THE EXCITING THING about hospitality is that your menu can always be refined and improved upon. Because food trucks have limited menus, it is relatively simple to adjust menus on the fly.

Studying Menu Mix

What are your customers actually buying? Are there categories of goods you just aren't selling? Watch your menu mix daily, weekly, and monthly. You'll be surprised about what you might learn about your customers in different neighborhoods by their eating patterns. By knowing what moves in different locations, you can adjust your inventory so you'll have the appropriate amount of product. It might also give you inspiration for new specials; for example, if your vegetarian items go quickly in a certain part of town, try out a new vegan item there for the first time. It might end up becoming popular in other locations.

Also, pay keen attention to categories. If you aren't selling many drinks in a certain location, watch your customers' behaviors and ask them about it. If they get free drinks at the office, you'll never be able to compete with that, but if your customers are stopping at a convenience store to buy soda for 25 cents less on the way back to work, you might want to consider cutting your prices to avoid losing that sale.

Actual COGS versus Theoretical COGS

At the end of each month, you should compare the month's COGS with your theoretical COGS and the previous month's COGS. If there are changes, you will need to drill down to understand why. Produce is seasonal, so costs may change as different, vegetables come into season and go out of season. If particular ingredients are going up in cost, you might need to increase the price of the menu item, find a substitute for the ingredient, or drop the item from the menu.

Cost/Margin Menu Analysis

Hospitality professionals have come up with a number of ways to analyze a menu, but this is one of my personal favorites. It will take you a bit of time to plug all of this information into a spreadsheet, but the insight it will give you into your menu will be invaluable. I was first introduced to cost/margin menu analysis by the book *Menu Pricing and Strategy* by Jack Miller and David Pavesic. The goal is to examine all of your menu items based on their food cost and their weighted contribution margins. Food cost is the cost of goods sold for the item divided by the sales price.

$$COGS = Food + Paper$$

$$\%COGS = COGS/Sales\ Price$$

The contribution margin is the dollar value of the COGS subtracted from the COGS. The weighted contribution margin multiplies the contribution margin by the number of sales per period.

$$Net\ Contribution = Sales\ Price - COGS$$

$$Weighted\ Net\ Contribution = \#Sold \times (Sales\ Price - COGS)$$

Cost/margin analysis is very powerful because it incorporates a number of factors including food cost, profitability, popularity, and contribution margin into one framework. By breaking your menu down into a two by two matrix divided by average food cost and average contribution, you can hone in on the performance of each menu item.

Miller and Pavesic describe these categories as follows:

- Prime: low COGS, high contribution
- Standard: high COGS, high contribution

- Sleeper: low COGS, low contribution
- Problem: high COGS, low contribution

Based on the attributes of the category a menu item is included in, you're offered clear, prescriptive advice on how to improve the productivity of the menu items.

- **Primes:** These are menu items that have a low cost of goods sold and are contributing a lot to the economic viability of your business. Because these items are popular and in demand, they are what you might want all your customers eating. Steer customers toward these menu items, and be sure to maintain the quality and portion of these menu items. These items should have a prominent location on your menu. If you're feeling adventurous, you might consider raising prices a bit to test whether customers are willing to pay more, but in general these items are doing well, so you might want to leave well enough alone.
- **Standards:** These items are popular and contribute a lot to your business, but they are relatively expensive from a cost perspective. You might be able to earn more from these items by increasing prices slightly or lowering portions. Another option might be to try and find substitute ingredients that are less expensive so that you can maintain the price and lower the costs.
- **Sleepers:** These items have a low cost, but they don't sell enough to add much value to your business. Try to promote these items by giving them more prominent placement on the menu or by renaming them. It might be possible these items are overpriced and thus not selling, so you could lower the price to see if that increases sales.
- **Problems:** Items that are both expensive to make and don't sell well are always a problem. Since the standard options of raising the price or lowering the cost with less expensive ingredients might make them even less interesting to customers, a good strategy is to try to develop substitutes. If you cannot make this item work, you should take it off the menu. Especially on a food truck with limited space, all the menu items need to pull their weight.

Social Media

ONE OF THE major drivers of interest in food trucks has been improved technology that lets customers track trucks geographically over time. Finding a favorite food truck is a bit of a scavenger hunt, which adds to the fun and dynamism of eating on the streets. Social media is going to be an extremely important component of your business. According to a September 2011 National Restaurant Association survey, 13 percent of people who visited a food truck found out about it through social media (www.restaurant.org/nra_news_blog/2011/09/food-trucks-gaining-momentum-new-research-finds.cfm).

The Basics

In order to keep your brand top of mind with your customers, you need to give customers a reason to stay connected with your brand. The location of your truck is just the start. Share music, recipes, photos, articles, and run promotions to keep customers engaged.

- **Facebook** (facebook.com) is the largest social network on the Web. Facebook allows businesses to set up pages. Facebook is well suited to announcements and thematic discussion topics. A good way to use your Facebook page might be to share recent press or to set up polls about new menu items.
- **Twitter** (twitter.com) is a great way to build a base of followers and keep them updated. Since it is easily accessible on mobile devices, many food truck owners use it daily to update their locations and make it easier for people to find them. Keep in mind that tweets must be brief (140 characters or fewer). The Twitter @reply

and retweet functions are relatively reliable and offer easy ways to keep track of interactions with customers and conversations. The Twitter search tool is also a great way to find posts regarding your company or industry that may not be directed at you and gives you the opportunity to jump into the conversation.

- **Foursquare** (foursquare.com) allows people to use their smartphones to "check in" at various locations. It is another way to help your customers track you down, and it helps you set up special offers that reward your most loyal fans and followers. The person who checks in most often at any location earns the designation of "mayor" at that location. If you give your mayor special discounts, your customers may compete to see who can check in most frequently.
- **HootSuite** (hootsuite.com) aggregates all of the interactions for Facebook, Twitter, and Foursquare (as well as LinkedIn, Ping [a social media music site], and Myspace). You can use HootSuite to limit the number of services and posts you need to monitor.

Measuring and Monitoring

There is more to social media than simply being on Twitter or Facebook. To get the most out of the relationship, it is important to measure and monitor your engagement with your fans online. By measuring customer feedback to different types of engagement, you'll be able to refine what works best for your business.

Social media trackers are tools that can be used to measure the social media reaction toward your food truck. These tools allow you to track positive and negative reactions and match them with your actions, like running a promotion or vending at a particular location. There are three terms that are important to understand when it comes to social media monitoring or "tracking."

1. **Influence:** This term refers to the size and activity of the network of a particular social media user. For example, how many followers do you have? How many people retweet your posts? How many sites link to your blog? How many people comment on your blog posts?
2. **Sentiment:** This term refers to the general "mood" of the information available about your company through social media. Plainly

put, are people saying positive or negative things about your company? While many social media trackers will try to judge this automatically, they are frequently inaccurate, so you should stay engaged with your customers to check the information on your own.

3. **Volume:** This simply measures the number of times a specific phrase or keyword is mentioned. Many tools have the ability to create charts based on the volume for a keyword, which allows a company to track whether its actions have an impact.

Monitoring Tools

Here are a few monitoring tools to help you keep abreast of the dialogue about your brand. Please don't treat this as an exhaustive list. Since social media is such a new industry, these services are constantly changing, and new ones are constantly being added.

- **Google Alerts:** The alerts function of Google search (google.com/alerts) is one of the easiest to set up and use. It sends an e-mail alert with new index results on search terms—such as your truck's name or type of food (e.g., kogi, Korean BBQ). This will alert you when new content appears that will also be appearing to your customers (blog posts, articles, etc.).
- **Google Trends:** Another simple function from Google (google.com/trends) allows you to view a chart of the volume of searches for a selected keyword—a company name or other indicator, for example. This is a great way to monitor Internet reactions to company actions, such as promotions.
- **Google Analytics:** If you've built a website, Google Analytics (google.com/analytics) is a free tool to help determine where website traffic is coming from. Sign up via Google accounts and embed the Analytics HTML code on your website. The reports let you track where visitors are referred from, how long they stay, which pages they visit, the percentage of visitors who enter the site and leave without clicking anything (the "bounce rate"), and the language and location demographics of your visitors. Also important for food truck websites is the ability to see how many users are accessing the site from mobile devices or Wi-Fi hot spots (if they are accessing the site on the go).

- **Facebook Insights** (facebook.com/insights) offers a free service that tracks and charts gains and losses of "Likes" (people who are fans of your page) as well as interaction with your page. Most important among the functions are the abilities to view totals and monthly increases and decreases (in percentages) for Likes and active users, and post views and interactions. You can then analyze this data to determine which actions resulted in more Likes or which posts gained the most interaction from fans, thus keeping fans on the page and engaging in conversation. Additionally, Insights gives information about individual fans, indicating what cities/countries fans are from and which of the Facebook page "tabs" (such as Info, Photos, or any custom tabs) visitors click on. It also gives other information on the demographics of fans (age, gender) as well as information on referrals—that is, how visitors get to your Facebook page (a Google search, a Twitter link, etc.). This gives you information on how to design and promote your Facebook page and also knowledge about the geographical scope of your fan base.
- **Klout** (klout.com) is a free service that analyzes data from Twitter, LinkedIn, and Facebook to measure "influence," based on size of a user's network and frequency of interaction with the user. In addition to allowing users to see their influence in the form of a "Klout score," it also allows them to see which topics they are most influential about, as well as the same information for competitors.
- **Social Mention** (socialmention.com) is a tool that combines all the user-generated information about a topic into one chronological feed. It states that it aggregates over 100 sources including Facebook, YouTube, Twitter, Digg, Google, and so forth. You simply search a term, like the name of your business, and it helps give you a sense of the social media reactions to your brand.
- **IceRocket** (icerocket.com) is another similar aggregation tool with slightly different options. It offers searches from several different sources—blogs, Twitter, Facebook, video sites like YouTube, and image sites like Flickr. IceRocket has a "trend terms" tool that allows you to enter as many as five search terms and track/compare their popularity on blogs so you can see how your food truck stacks up against the competition.

- **Addict-o-matic** (addictomatic.com) is one of the most thorough trackers. It is free and allows you to create a permanent custom "page" for a search term with small boxes for each information source that you can rearrange as you wish.
- **Trackur** (trackur.com) gets material from a variety of sources including mainstream news sites, blogs, videos (including YouTube), images (including Flickr), Twitter, Reddit, and Delicious. You can search terms to see the most recent 100 mentions with influence scores. Trackur doesn't measure sentiment.
- **BoardReader** (boardreader.com) provides search result information from message boards and forums and basic tools for analysis of search volume (graphs that track popularity of a term in a year/month/week). BoardReader scans message boards relevant to food truck owners like the City Data, Chowhound, and RealFood forums.

Responding to Posts

The goal of these tabs is to track the conversations that are happening about your brand across multiple platforms so you can stay engaged and participate in shaping the dialogue of your truck. In general, it is a great strategy to always stay engaged with fans. Make an effort to be active on social media sites at least once daily so your dialogue is timely. Your posts should reinforce your brand. When there are positive mentions of your truck, reinforce them. Retweet, share a story, or open a dialogue.

If there are negative mentions of your brand, it is more complicated. If the posts are by an angry poster who is always critical or on a site that is generally critical of your brand, it is best to just let it be. Generally, the only times to engage with negative posts are if the facts are materially wrong, such as misquoted ingredients or incorrect pricing, or if it was a customer who had a bad experience and you want to correct the problem, such as a complaint that the food was cold. In these cases, you want to offer the customer a chance to come in and get a new meal.

Never misrepresent yourself or your affiliation with your business. This is commonly referred to as shilling. The Internet is based on trust, and shilling undermines the integrity of the websites you are posting on.

Connecting with Customers

WHILE SOCIAL MEDIA is important, the core of the food truck experience happens on the street. Twitter and Facebook alone don't build a business. Having a fun, accessible brand is a solid foundation, but your brand is going to ultimately be built on the service experiences that your guests have when they visit the truck. The experience of buying food outdoors on the street is part of the allure of food trucks. It is essential to embrace the chaos and openness of the street and make the most of it when interacting with guests.

Smile

This is the most important thing you can do to improve sales. People tend to mirror one another, so if you're smiling, they will smile. And who isn't happy when they are smiling and eating good food? Part of eating on the street is that it is more open and engaged. Because the street is public space, it is a community experience. Don't be shy about smiling at people on the street, waving, or saying, "Hi!"

Recognize Regulars

Especially in urban areas, as more and more people crowd into smaller spaces, there has been a decline in the sense of community. Recognizing regulars shows a keen attention to detail and builds a lasting relationship. If you recognize a customer who has come a few times, introduce yourself. Happy customers lead to repeat sales and often to better tips!

Secret Surprises!

According to one of my cashiers who is getting a Master's degree in psychology, the best way to reinforce a behavior is "random, intermittent, positive reinforcement." Basically, this means you should somewhat randomly give your customers a really exciting treat just for being your customer. Try to think of something fun and interesting that you can tuck into your customer's bag as they check out. Maybe a piece of homemade caramel or a freshly baked cookie. It is important that it is off the menu so it doesn't have a price associated with it. Just make them feel a little special. A little special can go a long way toward building a lasting relationship with your customers.

When to Use "Free"

The best way to give things away for free is when they are unexpected. A free gift builds a lot of positive effect. When you first start vending in a new neighborhood, bring an extra employee so you can leave the truck to run free food up to the local offices or into local businesses. Introduce yourself and leave a card. Be sure to meet receptionists as they are often the information hub of the office and will let others know where you're located. Another great time to offer free food is at the end of your shift. If you have prepared product that cannot be stored, don't throw it away; instead, give the last three or four portions to whoever passes by next and invite them to come back if they liked the food.

Have a Phone Number

While social media is hot, don't overlook traditional ways to connect with guests, such as a phone number. Many offices block employee access to Twitter and Facebook, so if these are the only means your customers have to contact you, then they may not be able to find you. Record a message daily that gives your location so that customers can call in to find out where you are. This phone number doesn't need to be an actual line: You can get a number that goes directly to voicemail from many services, including Google Voice, for free.

Advertising

Advertising? Don't do it. When it comes to restaurants, people trust word of mouth more than any other source. Food trucks cannot compete with the advertising budgets of national chains. Your goal is to win customers over one at a time on the street.

Promotion

Personally, I am a big fan of value. Entrepreneurs should strive to provide great service and great value for each and every meal that they serve. If you'd like to run a promotion, I'd encourage you to run deals that reward loyalty. Acquiring new customers is much more expensive than retaining existing customers. Do everything you can to keep customers once you have them.

Seasonality

THE CHANGING SEASONS can make food truck vending very hard. Truckers in markets with more temperate climates definitely have an advantage because the extremes of a hot summer and a cold winter can make operating very challenging.

Should You Stay Open?

In the Northeast, the winter cuts sales for savory trucks about 30 percent. Every truck is different, so you may need to run your truck during a slow season in order to know how it will perform in the future. The first thing to keep in mind is your profitability. In order to stay open for a slow season, you'll want a reasonable degree of confidence that you can breakeven or eke out a bit of profit. The next thing to consider is your stakeholders. If you serve coffee, which is a very habitual food, you may not want to disappear on your regulars for a season, because they might create a new routine, going somewhere else for their daily coffee. Also, if members of your team want the stability of working year-round, it might be a good idea to stay open just to keep them paid in the off-season so you have a talented and experienced team ready for your next busy season.

Watch Your Cash

If you decide to go for it and work through a slow season, the first thing you should consider is your cash. You should go into your slow season knowing that sales are going to drop and that profitability is going to drop. You might even end up losing a bit of money. Do not get caught by surprise and run out of cash. It is good to plan ahead in the summer and get a line of credit and maybe even apply for a small loan to help you manage your cash flow through the winter.

Menu Mix

As the weather changes, your menu should change. Have seasonal items. In the winter, focus on warm food like soups or feature warm drinks like hot chocolate. Also, watch produce prices. As different vegetables come into season, their prices will drop. This is a great opportunity for you to keep your menu fresh and interesting while keeping your costs under control.

Quality Control

As the weather gets colder, fewer and fewer customers are willing to leave their offices to grab a snack, especially if it involves waiting in line outdoors. As business slows in the winter, it is important to ensure that operations on the truck don't suffer. Keep an eye on product quality and slow down operations to make all the products to order to ensure freshness. It is important to check all your inventory pars for ordering and to prep on the truck. If your staff preps food to summer pars, you will have a lot of waste, which will drive up your food cost.

Snow

Snow presents a number of special challenges for food trucks. Snow can significantly limit the number of customers willing to visit your truck, so your first decision should be whether it is even worth being open. If you are vending at the bottom of a ski slope in Colorado, a snowy day could be ideal. If it is the first snow in years in your town in Florida, it is a great day to stay off of the roads.

Driving in the snow doesn't come naturally to everyone. Be sure that anyone on your staff who will be driving in the snow has experience. If you are vending in the snow, be sure to shovel a path to the vending window.

Maintenance

KEEPING YOUR TRUCK well maintained is essential to running a profitable food truck business. One extremely challenging aspect to food trucks is that whenever a truck needs to be brought in for a repair, the opportunity to vend for the day is lost. Unplanned maintenance or breakdowns can not only ruin a shift but can also jeopardize long-term relationships with customers. Here is a quick guide to preventive maintenance for your truck, generator, and kitchen equipment.

Truck Maintenance

- **Oil changes:** Suggestions include checking your oil every 5,000 miles if you're driving in extreme weather conditions, driving an older vehicle, or carrying large amounts of equipment or a crew.
- **Fluid level checks:** Rather than relying on the various lights and buzzers that indicate low levels, it's suggested that you check these by hand on a fairly regular basis.
- **Rotating tires:** Rotate about every 5,000 miles. A mechanic can make sure they're inflated to their proper PSI, improving gas mileage and the safety of those on the truck.
- **Tune-ups:** A modern tune-up is less involved than the traditional one from half a century ago, but it is still worth having a professional mechanic test the brakes and battery, run full department of transportation inspections, and everything else that comes with a thorough tune-up.
- **Crew upkeep:** It's worth relying on a couple of members of the truck to check conditions out regularly. They should be trained to know what needs to be checked and have the tools to do so.

- **Supplies for breakdowns:** It's a good idea to have tools onboard for easy fixes. These include jumper cables, an extra quart of oil, a funnel, and a tool kit. You may want to find your own source for truck parts. Mill Supply (millsupply.com) specializes in step van parts.
- **Insurance:** Always have the right coverage for every one of your trucks. You have to be ready for any risk that's facing your fleet.

Generator Maintenance

Always read the instructions that come with your generator. Learn the part numbers for the oil filters, fuel filters, and air filters, and keep a few extra on hand all the time. Changing the oil is relatively simple, but the rules surrounding disposing of oil are often complex because of the environmental impact. For that reason, it might make sense to have a mechanic change the oil for you. Your truck mechanic might be able to do your oil changes for you, so you can take your truck in routinely to get an oil change for the truck and the generator at the same time. Once you figure out the rate at which you are using the truck, you should preschedule oil changes for a slow day.

Equipment Maintenance

Always read the instructions that come with your kitchen equipment. Make sure it is installed in a way so that it is easy to access and clean. Be sure to do routine maintenance like cleaning air filters on fridges and freezers. Most kitchen equipment wasn't designed to be used on a food truck. The constant motion and rattling from driving means that the equipment breaks down more frequently than it might in a restaurant. So baby your equipment. Do any required maintenance more frequently than you might for in a store. If there are parts that are consistently breaking, buy spare parts and learn how to change them on your own. Also, start searching for more durable equipment as you'll want to have your research done so you can do a quick swap when the equipment gives out for good.

Grow: Moving beyond the Truck

SOME ENTREPRENEURS ARE looking for a single truck; others are hoping to have more. The following section examines important considerations in growing a mobile food chain and diversifying from mobile food into brick-and-mortar restaurants and wholesale. In the following pages we'll also briefly examine licensing and franchising. Also, what are the possible exit strategies for a food truck entrepreneur? Is a food truck brand ever worth more than the value of its assets?

Interview 6: Natasha Case of Coolhaus on Growing Her Food Truck Business

Coolhaus is the first gourmet branded truck with a national reach. Coolhaus operates four trucks and a shop in Los Angeles, two trucks in Austin, two trucks and a cart in New York City, and two trucks in Miami. They also have a successful retail product that they sell in Whole Foods Market.

Q: What are the best and worst things about street vending?

The best thing about street vending is the creativity and flexibility that food trucks allow. Food trucks allow entrepreneurs to breathe new life into old food concepts. They can take risks that brick-and-mortar restaurants cannot. Food trucks are on the cutting edge of innovation in hospitality. They are all about enthusiasm and adventure. The uncertainty is the hardest thing about food truck vending. The trucks are very prone to break down and we have repairs almost every week. It is challenging to stay on top of breakdowns. Having trucks that cannot vend puts a big strain on management and overhead. We just opened a brick-and-mortar shop in Los Angeles. The shop is much easier to oversee because everything is stable. Because they are remote, trucks need to rely on technology and honesty.

Q: What was your biggest lesson after you started street vending?

We started April 2009. The first lesson we learned was how to manage production. When we were first selling we made both the cookie and the ice cream for our ice cream sandwiches. We knew we'd need a better means of production if we wanted to grow because we didn't have the resources at our commissary in Pasadena. We went to copacking at the start. We reached out to a number of copackers for custom cookies and ice cream. We've built up great relationships for suppliers who can grow with us.

(continued)

(continued)

Q: What is one thing you would recommend to someone thinking of opening a truck?

Take the time to do your research. There is an illusion that you can start with nothing and make a fortune. There is oversaturation in the market in Los Angeles. I see trucks opening who aren't putting enough forethought into developing their business, their brand, and their clientele. Before an entrepreneur opens a truck they should ask themselves, am I different enough? Success on the road is about brand building.

Q: How have your operations had to change in different markets?

As we've gone to more cities, the biggest change has been developing our corporate team. The primary change has been more management with specific expertise. We have an executive pastry chef who oversees our food production to be sure that things are being done properly. We now have opening teams who are specialists in the food industry and who have experience opening new markets to train the initial team in each city.

Q: What is your process to open to new markets?

As we go to more cities we are learning the right questions to ask at the start of the process to discern what is different about each market. Over time you build up better intuition. We ask about health regulation codes as they pertain to our product right at the start. It's also important to learn where municipal boundaries end. A suburb outside a city might seem tempting, but even though the demographics are good, the reason no one is vending there is because the regulations are different and don't allow you to operate. Developing a start-up manual has improved our launch process. Even though the rules are different, most of what we do is the same each time. We're planning to open in San Francisco this spring. People know us in San Francisco, so it will be easier than in Miami.

Q: What market has been the hardest to operate in?

New York City is the craziest. The fact that you can be arrested for not having a mobile food-vending badge is unbelievable. Just take a moment to think about going to jail for making an ice cream sandwich. Where does that happen? Only in New York City. We are licensed by the NYC Deptartment of Parks to vend in Central Park, and the NYPD comes almost weekly to try and shut us down. New York City has extremely strict laws, and there is a lot more vendor-versus-vendor conflict in NYC, but because there are so many people, there is also more money to be made.

Q: How long did you work the trucks until you hired more staff?

I left my other job a month after we started, so I was on the truck full time for a year. As we grew, I spent less time on the truck and more time developing the brand and managing the growth of the company.

Q: What types of technology do you use to manage your business?

We use a POS system to see product mix. We originally set up the Paysaver POS just to use it for processing credit cards. Over time we started using more of the features, and having access to the product mix is very useful. In the store there are security cameras. We haven't quite figured out how to do that on the truck yet. However, we use social media to keep tabs on our operations. We ask customers about their experiences and to send photos of their favorite sandwiches. We see photos posted on Twitter and feedback from Yelp. If the sandwich looks melted or doesn't have the right proportions, we can follow up with the team that served it to ensure quality and consistency.

Q: What incentives do you use?

We give bonuses to corporate staff for meeting financial goals. We give a commission for sales for private events. We do pay more than most trucks. We pay from $13 to $15 per hour in Los Angeles, and I think we get what we pay for. However, more than paying high wages or bonuses, we try to make our team feel like they are a part of something important and that what they do matters. It is very important that our team feels appreciated.

(continued)

(continued)

Q: How did Coolhaus end up licensing the brand so early?

We were approached by people from Austin to license the Coolhaus brand. Our original plan was to go to New York because we were more familiar with the market. Austin was interesting because it was an opportunity to try a new market without taking the capital risk. The Austin trucks are now owned by Coolhaus again because the licensees moved on. However, it was a good experiment and it gave us the opportunity to grow at a time when we couldn't have otherwise. Ultimately, the whole situation worked out well, but we probably tried to do too much too early. We could have let the company mature. At the point we did the Austin licensing deal we didn't even have a lawyer. Managing a licensee or a franchise is hard to do unless you are in the franchise business. There is much more involved than you might expect.

Q: What did you learn through the licensing process?

Trying to explain how to run a Coolhaus truck to someone on the other side of the country made us realize how much of the business was in our heads. It triggered us to write all our manuals. When we made the deal we weren't working with the copacker as we are now, and we didn't have the ability to ship them our ice cream. They were producing their own ice cream to our specifications locally, but it was impossible to supervise the product. In general, it was a nightmare. If you are taking your brand national, having central hubs of production is essential. In every market we also have locally made items.

Q: How has selling at Whole Foods Market helped your brand?

The transition from food trucks to wholesale was relatively seamless because we already had our copacking relationships in place. It is becoming more important financially as the scope of the distribution of our products increases. At the beginning we were in three Whole Foods and it was almost more work than it was worth. We were putting so much time and effort into it for such limited revenue, it didn't make much financial sense. However, there are some nonquantifiable aspects to having your product in Whole Foods. It shows the legitimacy of your product to your customers in that it meets the Whole Foods criteria of being natural, healthful, and sanitary. Now we are in 22 Whole Foods Markets in southern California and it really contributes to the business.

Q: How is running a restaurant different from running a food truck?

The Coolhaus store was a way to capitalize on those customers in Los Angeles who don't use Facebook or Twitter or don't want to chase down a food truck. Start-up costs are a lot more, but for us the profit margins are actually better. We use the store as our corporate headquarters and the base for all the Los Angeles food truck operations.

Growth Opportunities

More Owner-Operated Trucks

Perhaps the most logical way to grow your business is to open more trucks. In many ways this is the next logical step to develop your brand. Once you have figured out the local rules and a smooth operational process to run your truck profitably, the hurdles to get the next truck started are a lot lower. However, food trucks don't scale well, and there are a few challenges to keep in mind as you grow. First, as the owner, you can only be in one place at a time. With two trucks, you'll need to pick and choose where to spend your time to add the most value. As you leave the operations, you'll find that certain things that you used to do on a daily or weekly basis may no longer be getting done. This is why documenting the daily, weekly, and monthly responsibilities is so important.

As you add more trucks to your fleet, you may not be able to maintain the revenue per truck of your initial truck. If your city allows street vending, you probably have your first truck in all the best locations you've found over time, which means the second truck will be allocated to the second best location you can find each day. Also, having two trucks doesn't mean you are invited to cater twice as many weddings or visit twice as many movie sets. Your catering and special event sales will probably drop with your second truck. The second truck will allow you to do two catering events on the same night, but that won't happen all the time. Also, as you have more trucks, the time you can spend on any particular truck drops. The connection you have with regulars needs to be passed along to other members of the team. When customers visit a food truck, it makes a big difference if they can chat with the owner. Your employees can be trained to represent the business very well, but there is always something special about being recognized and thanked by the owner.

Owning multiple trucks may improve your cost structure slightly in regard to food costs, paper costs, insurance costs, or occupancy. As you have bigger accounts with your vendors, they may be able to cut you a few breaks here and there. However, food trucks are small operations in the grand scheme of most hospitality businesses, so you shouldn't expect prices to drop much as you grow. One area in which you might see costs increase as you grow is maintenance. Food trucks run by employees tend to require more maintenance. Without oversight, employees may take shortcuts or be less careful with equipment.

If you are street vending, you may find that it is very hard to get your truck parked exactly where you want it to be. Your employees may not be as incentivized as you might be to get your first choice spot at the corner. Rather than wait for the best spot or ask a delivery van to move, they might settle for an isolated spot in the middle of the street. Picking good locations to vend and getting parked is hard work that is best suited to an owner.

Some entrepreneurs believe that the correct number for multiple trucks in one market is two. That gives you a primary strong earning truck and then a second truck so you don't miss out on events or catering opportunities when multiple opportunities arise on the same day. Also, it offers a bit of insurance in that if one truck breaks down, there is still a backup to keep revenue coming in on a daily basis, to keep employees busy, and to fulfill obligations to cater special events.

As you consider opening multiple trucks you should think about how to mitigate some of the common challenges to growth, what you want to be doing each day, and if your market is well suited to multiple trucks of the same type or if you might want to try a new concept for your second truck.

Running multiple trucks will require a change in the types of activities you do as an entrepreneur. Rather than operating a truck efficiently, you will be working on getting others to operate your trucks effectively. A great resource for help running multiple restaurant units that is easily transferred to the food truck industry is *Multi Unit Leadership* by Jim Sullivan. This is a great resource, both for you as an entrepreneur and for any future hires who will oversee multiple units of your business.

Licensing and Franchising Your Truck Concept

Another opportunity for growth is by licensing or franchising your food truck concept. In many ways licensing or franchising makes a lot of sense in this industry because it pays to have someone who truly cares about the business operating each truck. Since your licensee or franchisee will be operating the trucks, generally you can expect the revenues to be slightly better and the trucks to be a bit better run.

However, because of the low barriers to entry to the food truck market in general, many entrepreneurs might like to have their own business, so you'll need to have a plan for an operation that is extremely profitable and extremely reproducible so that there is enough value created for you to take your cut in fees and for the licensee or franchisee to still make a compelling living. Franchises typically charge an up-front training fee in addition to the costs of the truck, plus a 4 to 6 percent franchise fee off gross revenues and an additional 1 to 2 percent revenue fee. There is also an opportunity to earn a small premium on the food sold to the truck.

In order to license or franchise your business you'll need the assistance of a franchise lawyer to help you set up your business. This legal work can cost between $15,000 and $25,000. You'll also need to fully document how your operations are run. A good place to start your search is with Harold L. Kestenbaum, Esq. (franchiseatty .com), who has literally written the book on franchising: *So You Want to Franchise Your Business*. You'll also need thorough manuals and training guides to support new franchisees. There are franchise services that can help you through this process like ifranchise.com or francorp.com. These services can cost between $25,000 and $50,000. Some also look to collect a portion of the franchising revenue stream in the future.

New Markets

If you feel you have saturated the market you're in, you might want to expand your operation to another city or municipality. Before expanding your operation from New York City to Boston or Philly, look to other municipalities outside where you have typically been vending. You might be able to expand your operations to an office park in suburbs outside the city or to a college campus in a nearby town and still use the same commissary facilities. As you grow it is important to keep your revenues growing faster than your costs, so you should leverage any assets you've developed. While having an established brand and a smooth operation might help you get started in a new city, you'll be building the foundation of the business from scratch. You might even be at a disadvantage compared to other entrepreneurs who came out of the hospitality industry in that city and are more knowledgeable about the local regulations and have stronger relationships with local vendors.

Brick-and-Mortar Restaurants

Over time, you may come to long for the safety and stability of a restaurant. On hot days, you will long for a store with air conditioning; on rainy days, you will long for a store with indoor seating. Food truck operators have three big advantages over entrepreneurs who start restaurants without trucks: First, they have an established brand with existing fans of their food; second, they have an understanding of the economics of their business and a working business model; and third, they know where their customers are. It is important to keep these three things in mind and make the most of them as you grow into a restaurant space. It is very important to pick a location for your first restaurant that you know works. Use your truck to do research. If you cannot make good revenue selling off a truck, customers aren't going to magically appear when you open a store. The economics of brick-and-mortar restaurants are very similar to food trucks, but they are different in important ways. The opening costs tend to be higher and the fixed costs are higher, but the revenue is much higher as well. Be sure to rigorously examine the numbers of a restaurant. Talk with other contractors or entrepreneurs about the cost of the build and research the sales that other restaurants are doing in the area. Unlike a food truck, you cannot simply drive away if sales aren't working for the day, so be sure it is a location that will thrive for the entire duration of the lease.

Wholesale

Depending on the type of food you sell, it is possible to develop a branded product to sell wholesale. You will need a product that can be packaged to sell in retail shops. Coffee, cookies, cupcakes, dumplings, empañadas, ice cream, or ice cream sandwiches could all be sold wholesale. The margins for wholesale aren't great, but what you will ultimately have access to is a much larger market.

Wholesaling is a very different business model from street vending and requires a different set of skills. You will no longer be selling directly to the consumers of your product but to food buyers for grocery stores and specialty stores. The success of your product will be dictated by packaging, taste, and value.

If you are selling to retailers, not only will you be regulated by your local health department, but your production facilities will also need to be USDA-compliant. USDA regulations are generally much more rigorous. Depending on the existing infrastructure of your commissary kitchen, it might be necessary to upgrade to a better kitchen space or to have your product made by a copacker, a company that specializes in producing food products to spec for another company.

The wholesale supply chain generally moves from a manufacturer to a distributor to a retail outlet to a consumer. The manufacturer generally aims to make a margin of 40 to 45 percent. However, if you are using a copacker, your margin will probably be a bit lower. The distributor acts as an intermediary to inventory multiple products and deliver consolidated orders to the retail outlet. The distributor needs to make a margin of 25 to 30 percent to cover the costs of warehousing and distributing the product. The retail outlet stocks and sells your product to consumers. They usually require a margin of 35 to 40 percent to cover the costs of their rent and labor and to make a small profit.

Let's say you sold a product for $5.50 on your truck that had a cost of goods sold (COGS) of $1.60. On your truck this product would be a 29 percent food cost. Every one you sold would contribute $3.90 ($5.50 − $1.60) to help you cover all your labor, operational, and occupancy costs. If you were selling the same product wholesale, the economics might look something like the following table.

For everyone to get what they need out of the equation, it pushes the price up about $.50 above what it might have cost a customer to buy the same product on your truck. Depending on how your product scales, you might be able to lower the cost of goods sold if you are

Allocation of Value in the Retail Supply Chain

	COGS	Copacker	Manufacturer	Distributor	Retail Outlet	Consumer (SRP)
Sale Price	$ 1.60	$ 2.00	$ 2.67	$ 3.56	$ 5.93	$ 5.93
Purchase Price		$ 1.60	$ 2.00	$ 2.67	$ 3.56	
Gross		$ 0.40	$ 0.67	$ 0.89	$ 2.37	
Markup		25.0%	33.3%	33.3%	66.7%	
Margin		20.0%	25.0%	25.0%	40.0%	
Standard Margin		40–45%	25–30%	35–40%		

buying in bulk, which could push down the price to a level closer to what it sells for on your food truck. If you need to hit the $5.50 suggested retail price, it might be up to you as the manufacturer to concede some value.

It will be important for you to model the earning potential of wholesale products and whether there is enough volume to support the administrative costs of coordinating wholesale runs with a copacker, managing inventory, and promoting the product.

Contract Packing

A CONTRACT PACKER, or copacker, manufactures and packages food products to order. By moving the production of your food from in-house to a contract facility, you can increase the scale of your production, improve product consistency, potentially lower costs by ordering in bulk, and pack your food for retail sale. This chapter is an extremely brief examination of the copacking process. For a thorough look at the process of copacking, take a look at *New Food Product Development: From Concept to Marketplace* by Gordon Fuller. There are also a number of consulting services that can help you navigate the copacking process.

Does Copacking Work for Me?

Copacking works well for products that are made in volume and have a reasonable storage life. Almost any food product can be made to order. The first challenge you may run into as a food truck is scale. You'll need to be ordering in volumes large enough to make it worth it for a copacker to spend factory time switching over the line to run your product. To start, generally you'll need to find smaller food manufacturers. Make sure that the volumes you end up buying are affordable from a cash perspective. You don't want to lock all of your free cash up in inventory. Also, make sure that the inventory doesn't last longer than the shelf life of the goods you are purchasing.

Standard Operating Procedures

Assuming you can find a copacker that can make your product, you'll need to develop standard operating procedures (SOPs). SOPs are always done by weight so that the results are more consistent. If your recipes are already done by weight, you will have a head start in getting your SOPs developed. If your ingredients use branded ingredients, you may be able to save some money by recreating those flavors with commodity ingredients.

Finding a Copacker

Depending on your product it can be either very easy or very challenging to find a copacker that can make your product to spec. The best place to start your search for a copacker is via an association website or trade shows. One way to track down potential copackers for specialty items is to ask equipment manufacturers about their other clients. That will give you a short list of companies to approach.

Choosing a Copacker

Your most important priorities in choosing a copacker should be the quality and integrity of the operation. Is it clean and meeting all health and safety codes? Is it able to make the food to your specifications? Does the price work for you? You should first confirm that the copacker is able to produce your product. Usually, you can do this by phone, but going in person is even better. Are they making similar products? Do they have the right equipment? Are they USDA-certified? Will they be making the product themselves, not just brokering it out to another facility? Do they have basic food safety programs in place? What are their minimum run amounts? What sort of packaging options do they have?

When you have a short list of at least three vendors, you should arrange factory visits to get to know the people and facilities better. When you are on-site, confirm that their hazard analysis and critical control points (HACCP) plans are in place and that the facility, staff, sourcing, receiving, and warehousing all meet your expectations.

If you'd like to move forward be sure to get a signed nondisclosure agreement (NDA) to protect the intellectual property of your recipes and SOPs. Once you have a signed NDA, you can provide the copacker with the SOPs. The copacker will work from the SOPs to come up with a final version of the product. Once you have approved a refined SOP, they can fine-tune pricing and you can work out a final contract. Be sure to know the required minimums, the terms of delivery, the turn-around time from order to production, whether there are price breaks with volume, and the terms under which prices may be increased over time.

Oversight

You'll definitely want to participate in the production process until the copacker has fully earned your trust. Even then, you should do surprise spot checks and test every batch before it is delivered. Arrange to have samples sent to you or to a testing service like Shuster Labs now UL-STR; (strquality.com).

Distribution

A good distributor will make a big difference in your ability to sell your product. In addition to their cost structure, take a look at who their clients are. Make sure that they service retailers where your end users shop.

Building the Right Infrastructure

As YOUR COMPANY grows in size, you'll need additional infrastructure to support it. While you may have been able to work on the truck and do the books on Monday night when you had only one truck, with two trucks or four trucks, you simply won't have the time. It can be especially hard to do this if your company grows rapidly. A great book to consult on this topic is *No Man's Land: A Survival Manual for Growing Midsize Companies* by Doug Tatum.

Money

The cash crunch you were so worried about when you opened never really goes away. If you decide to grow, the investments you make will use a lot of cash. If you open a new truck, not only will you need to spend money on a new vehicle and training for staff, but you'll need to lock up more cash in inventory so you have enough food for both your trucks to run each day. If you are ordering from a copacker or starting, your inventory requirements might be even higher. Be sure that you have the resources you need in place before you start expanding.

Management Team

As your business grows, the types of people you'll need will change. If you're wholesaling, you may need a sales manager or a production coordinator. If you open a restaurant, you may need a general manager for that restaurant. If you open more trucks, you may need truck managers. Consider the roles you want to play in the business and where you add the most value. Hire around those constraints. Look for team

174

members with drive and dedication. If at all possible, look to hire and develop team members internally.

Organizational Structure

Entrepreneurial ventures are by definition extremely hierarchical. Initially, every decision will go through the founder. However, in time, responsibility for decision-making needs to be spread out to others in the organization. Plan ahead and know this transition is coming. Think about the best way for the business to be organized, and bring in people you can trust, people who share your goals and the mission for the business.

Shared Services

Think about the most efficient way to operate your business. If you have multiple types of businesses, you could save overhead costs by consolidating human resources, accounting, and billing.

Technology

As YOU MOVE to having multiple mobile units, being able to track the details of how they are being run while you are away from the trucks is extremely important.

Smartphones

Smartphones are amazing for food truck operations. If your team members have smartphones it is much easier to stay in touch with them and have them stay in touch with you. Camera phones are a huge help when you are away from the trucks as staff can photograph images of broken equipment or a parking challenge to better keep you abreast of the situation.

Online Scheduling

Online scheduling was touched upon earlier in the book. With one truck, an online schedule is optional, but with multiple trucks or an owner who is sometimes on the truck and sometimes working at a restaurant or overseeing copacking runs, having the schedule online can make a huge difference in operations on the fly. An online schedule that is updated every time employees change shifts is an incredibly important tool if you are trying to call the employee on a particular truck. Take a look at schedulefly.com, whentomanage.com, or hotschedules.com.

POS System

With multiple trucks you will really want a cloud-based POS system. Being able to check sales in real time is extremely important to manage your business effectively. By knowing what the sales are on a rainy day you can discern whether or not to close a shift. POS systems are also very helpful in detecting fraud. Because you can watch when transactions are happening, you can tell if employees are not ringing up items or if they are voiding items in slow periods and paying themselves out of the drawer. Two iPad-based systems worth taking a look at are Revel.com and Shopkeep.com.

GPS Tracking and Guidance

A global positioning system can be very helpful in tracking where your trucks are. To be safe (and in compliance with local law in many areas), your employees shouldn't be talking on cell phones while driving, so being able to see where they are in real time is extremely useful. This can be especially important when trucks are lost and looking for directions or if they are late for a special event and you need to give a customer an estimate of when the truck might arrive. Key decision criteria are functionality and price. Some differentiating factors for food trucks might be a Web-based system that can be checked on the move, the ability to view trucks via mobile Web or an app support, and the ability to access your geo-positioning data via an application programming interface (API) [if you want to put your truck's location on a website]. Some tracking systems will tie into a GPS navigation system, like a Garmin or TomTom GPS, that your drivers can use to find their way. For an additional fee, it is possible to set up a dispatch service where you can pass information between the navigation device and the website. One nice feature is the ability to push an address to the navigation device so you can direct your team to the nearest garage for a repair or to a special event that was just called in. Some companies that can help to start your search are nextraq.com, navtrak.net, and fleetmatics.com.

Mobile Surveillance

Surveillance systems are in place in almost every restaurant because they are extremely useful in discouraging theft by both patrons and employees. Surveillance systems can be very useful in training and ensuring compliance with company procedure. Being able to see what is going on in your truck when you aren't there is extremely valuable.

Ideally, many entrepreneurs would love to have access to this in real time. However, the major challenge with setting up real-time surveillance on food trucks is the bandwidth required to stream video data. It can be done, but it requires good wireless data speeds, usually 4G, and relatively expensive technology. A simpler solution is to set up a digital video recorder (DVR) to record video during the day and then download it wirelessly to a computer at your commissary at night. This will give you a one-day lag on your video, but you'll still have ready access to what happened on your trucks while you were away. A few companies are working on this issue, such as angeltrax.com, boundlesssecurity.com, and mobilewitness.com. To find others, search the term *mDVR*.

Exiting the Food Truck Industry

RUNNING A FOOD truck is hard work. It is physical and exhausting. And your sales are often subject to powerful forces outside your control, like the weather or local regulatory changes. Running a food truck can tire you out. If you get burned out, one option is to settle down your business and look for a more stable vending opportunity. The less moving parts there are, the simpler your operations will be. If you think you want to exit the food truck industry, you should plan ahead so that you can get the most value possible in selling your business.

Selling Your Business versus Selling Your Food Truck

The first thing you'll need to decide is if you want to sell your business, including the brand name, recipes, and operational instructions, or if you just want to sell your food truck. If you plan on using your brand or your product in a kiosk or in wholesale, you'll definitely want to hold onto all your intellectual property rights.

Generally, being able to sell a profitable business will earn you a higher sales price than just trying to sell the underlying assets, namely the truck and the kitchen equipment. To sell your business you'll need to make the operations as seamless as possible for the new buyer. Training materials will be very useful to get them up to speed. You should probably also plan to spend a few weeks transitioning the business over to them so that they can keep the momentum of the business going.

At the moment, many entrepreneurs entering the food truck industry want to set up their own businesses that reflect their own passions and creativity. Currently, it isn't easy to sell a food truck business

179

for more than the value of the assets themselves. As the food truck market matures, I believe that established food truck brands will command more and more value as franchises and as owner-operated businesses that new entrepreneurs might want to take over rather than start from scratch.

Before You Sell

Create a pitch book, not unlike the business plan outlined earlier in the book. Highlight the strengths of the operation relative to other competitors in the market. Show the strength of the brand by referencing material from social media tracking services. Also, include representative comments from customers received via e-mail, comment cards, or Twitter.

Get your financial house in order. Make sure all of your records are in order. Potential buyers will want to thoroughly review financials and take a look at supporting documentation, such as receipts and invoices.

Hone the operations: For example, make sure your training manuals are updated for how the operations are currently run and update recipes.

Setting a Price

When setting a price you'll want to come up with a number by looking at both the value of your business and the value of the underlying assets. In general, publicly traded restaurants sell at a multiple of something close to five times their revenue or seven times their earnings. You can check this by looking up a few publicly traded restaurant chains on finance.yahoo.com. When you look at the numbers of your business, keep in mind that publicly traded stocks typically sell for higher multiples than small start-ups because they are more stable and there is more trust in the numbers that they are publishing because they are subject to FCC oversight. Small operations have the promise of greater growth, but they are also more likely to fail and are thus riskier investments. Next take a look at what the value of the assets you have in your business. How much is your truck worth? How much is the kitchen equipment worth? Look for the prices of comparable used assets on Craigslist or on eBay™.

A good starting price is somewhere between the market value of the assets and the number you get by calculating the multiples. The more profitable and stable your business and the stronger your brand, the more likely you'll be to command a premium above the value of the assets. The speed with which you want to sell the business and the general state of the economy will also influence your pricing.

Afterword

THANK YOU FOR taking the time to read this book. I hope the information presented here is helpful in pursuing your mobile food venture. As you move forward, remember these key points, and your project is sure to benefit.

Take the time to do the research to come up with a viable business plan. The food truck market isn't going anywhere. There will always be a market for great food served at a great price, so don't rush.

Raise enough money. Most start-ups fail because they don't have the funds they need to get to a stable run-rate. Food trucks that are short on funds tend to act irresponsibly, cut corners on cleaning, and vend recklessly. Be sure to budget for an extra cushion to get started.

Vend responsibly. Treat your stakeholders with respect. Remember that you are part of a larger community of food truck vendors. By vending responsibly, we can improve the industry and make lasting, positive contributions to the communities where we work.

Share your experiences opening your food truck with me so that together we can improve future editions of this book and provide aspiring food truck entrepreneurs the information and tools they need to run profitable businesses that contribute to the local community.

www.foodtrucker.info

Appendix A
Templates and Worksheets

Starting Expenses Template

Truck Asset Costs	Low	Medium	High
Step Van	$5,000	$20,000	$120,000
Mechanic Inspection	$100	$400	$500
Fabricator Fees	$20,000	$25,000	$50,000
Kitchen Equipment	$5,000	$10,000	$20,000
Generator	$2,000	$6,000	$12,000
Painting	$1,500	$2,000	$3,000
Truck Wrap	$2,000	$2,500	$3,500
Misc			
Truck Subtotal	$35,600	$65,900	$209,000
Preopening Expenses	**Low**	**Medium**	**High**
Smallwares	$400	$500	$800
Register/POS	$200	$1,000	$2,000
Licenses/Permits	$300	$500	$1,000
Phone/Internet	$100	$200	$250
Music	$100	$200	$300
Payroll Setup	$0	$100	$150
Office Setup	$100	$400	$800
Website	$2,000	$3,000	$8,000
Photography	$500	$1,000	$1,500
Menu Printing	$500	$750	$1,000
T-Shirts	$0	$250	$500
Fuel	$200	$250	$300
Ingredients (1wk/training)	$800	$1,000	$1,500
Paper Products (1wk/training)	$200	$250	$1,500
Labor (1wk/training)	$1,000	$1,500	$2,000
Misc			
Preopening Subtotal	$6,400	$10,900	$21,600
Misc	**Low**	**Medium**	**High**
Deposits	$500	$1,000	$2,000
Misc			
Misc Subtotal	$500	$1,000	$2,000
TOTAL	$42,500	$77,800	$232,600

Opening Timeline

Week	Category	Task	Owner	Complete
10	Administrative	Set up business as legal entity		
10	Commissary	Choose commissary location		
10	Food and Beverage	Finalize menu		
10	Licensing	Apply for all required licenses and permits		
10	Office	Set up office space		
10	PR/Marketing	Set up social media accounts for Facebook, Twitter, Foursquare, etc.		
10	Printer	Design menus, business cards, T-shirts, uniforms, etc.		
10	Signage	Truck exterior design		
10	Truck Construction	Purchase or rent a truck		
10	Truck Construction	Choose a fabricator		
9	Administrative	Register truck		
9	Administrative	Set up liability insurance, auto insurance		
9	Commissary	Review waste removal procedures and finalize carting		
9	Food and Beverage	Finalize kitchen equipment		
9	Kitchen Equipment	Finalize kitchen equipment		
9	Office	Order and schedule safe install		
9	Printer	Finalize and order take-out menus and business cards		
9	Truck Construction	Draft kitchen layout		
9	Truck Construction	Test kitchen layout		
8	Administrative	Establish credit sheet and vendor credit		

(continued)

Week	Category	Task	Owner	Complete
8	Administrative	Set up unemployment account		
8	Food and Beverage	Finalize recipes		
8	HR	Set up system to file employee paperwork		
8	Licensing	Receipts and posting of all permits		
8	Office	Tailor unit-specific documents		
8	Signage	Design exterior menu and press display		
8	Signage	Size and order menu board and frame		
8	Smallwares	Edit smallwares opening inventory		
8	Truck Construction	Spec out generator		
8	Truck Construction	Order generator		
7	Administrative	Choose register or POS		
7	Food and Beverage	Calculate theoretical food costs		
7	HR	Develop theoretical staffing schedule to determine number of staff to hire		
7	Office	Organize all electronic documents on cloud-based storage		
7	Signage	Order legal and health signs		
7	Smallwares	Price, bid on, and order smallwares		
6	Administrative	Purchase register or POS		
6	Food and Beverage	Set up ordering sheet and pars		
6	Office	Set up printer and fax		
5	Administrative	Set up new payroll account		
5	Administrative	Set up register or POS		

(continued)

Week	Category	Task	Owner	Complete
5	HR	Place ad locally for staff needs		
5	Kitchen Equipment	Receive kitchen equipment and file warranties		
5	Kitchen Equipment	Turn on and test all equipment		
5	Printer	Receive takeout menus and business cards		
5	Signage	Attain health department signage: decide on posting locales		
5	Smallwares	Receive smallwares		
4	Commissary	Hire prep staff if required		
4	HR	Begin interview process		
4	Licensing	Schedule health inspection		
4	Office	Delivery of safe		
4	Office	Key box with master keys		
4	PR/Marketing	Finalize and submit all hours of operation		
4	Smallwares	Finalize linens contract		
3	Commissary	Establish inventory storage system		
3	Commissary	Train food prep staff		
3	Commissary	Begin receiving nonperishable food items		
3	Commissary	Set up storerooms/metroshelves		
3	Food and Beverage	Set up storage		
3	HR	Hire		
3	HR	Finalize preopening training schedule dates		
3	PR/Marketing	Website update: hours, location, phone number, map, etc.		

(continued)

Week	Category	Task	Owner	Complete
3	Smallwares	Place opening paper products order		
2	Commissary	Big cleaning and setup of commissary space		
2	Food and Beverage	Place initial orders and receive food		
2	HR	Distribute schedule to staff: seven-day count		
2	Kitchen Equipment	Train opening team on equipment operation and troubleshooting		
2	Office	Submit information for first payroll		
2	Office	Employee telephone list (cell phones, etc.)		
2	PR/Marketing	Decide opening schedule		
2	PR/Marketing	Schedule photo shoot for truck		
2	Signage	Get truck painted or wrapped		
2	Signage	Receive in-store posters and promotional signage		
2	Smallwares	Schedule first linen delivery		
2	Smallwares	Receive paper		
2	Truck Construction	Truck construction complete		
1	HR	Whole-staff orientation day (all staff finish paperwork)		
1	PR/Marketing	Reach out to local press and food blogs about opening		
1	Signage	Sign day: install all signs, water, bathroom, CPR, etc.		
1	Signage	Install exterior menu and press display		
1	Smallwares	First linen delivery		
1	Smallwares	Set in place clean smallwares		

Credit Sheet Template

Credit Information
Company Name: _____
DBA: _____
Phone #: _____
Type of Business: _____
Date Established: _____
Number of Employees: _____
Federal Tax ID #: _____

Corporate Information
Officer's Name: _____
Address: _____
E-mail: _____
Phone: _____

Banks
Bank Name: _____
Address: _____
Phone: _____
Contact Person: _____
Account #: _____

Trade Credit
Company: _____
Address: _____
Sales Rep: _____
Phone: _____

Company: _____
Address: _____
Sales Rep: _____
Phone: _____

Company: _____
Address: _____
Sales Rep: _____
Phone: _____

Delivery Information
Contact: _____
Phone: _____
Address: _____
Delivery Times: _____

Notes: _____
_____
_____

Important Numbers Template

Emergencies

Company	Description	Name	Position	Contact	Notes
	Auto Insurance				
	Dept of Health				
	Disability				
	Fire				
	Liability Insurance				
	Mobile Food Advocacy				
	Police				
	Workmans Comp				

Vendors—Services/Supplies

Company	Description	Name	Position	Contact	Notes
	Bank				
	Commissary				
	Food Vendor				
	Kitchen Equipment				
	Paper Vendor				
	Payroll				
	POS Vendor				
	Propane Vendor				
	Truck Wraps				

Generator Repairs

Company	Description	Name	Position	Contact	Notes
	Generator Manufacturer				
	Generator Parts				
	Official Repair Company				

Kitchen Equipment Repairs

Company	Description	Name	Position	Contact	Notes
	Manufacturer				

Truck Repairs

Company	Description	Name	Position	Contact	Notes
	Auto Repair				
	Glass Repair				
	Roadside Repair				
	Step Van Parts				
	Tire Repair				
	Towing Service				
	Transmission Specialists					

Fellow Vendors

Company	Description	Name	Position	Contact	Notes

Goverment Offices

Department	Description	Name	Position	Contact	Notes

Schedule Template

Schedule Week of _____

Staff	Position	Monday	Tuesday	Wednesday	Thursday	Friday	Saturday	Sunday
Truck	Bfast							
	Lunch							
	Dinner							
Staff								

Order Sheet Template

Vendor Name: _____ *prices updated on:* _____

Sales Person & Contact Number: _____

Ordering Rules i.e. day before cutoff 3:45 PM, order Friday for Monday

Delivery Rules: M/W/F; $5 surcharge for orders < $200   *ordered by:* _____

Item	Code	Unit	Pack	Par	Price	Mon	Tue	Wed	Thurs	Fri	Sat	Sun
Item, 5# cs	1234	#	5	2								

Item	Code	Unit	Pack	Par	Price	Mon	Tue	Wed	Thurs	Fri	Sat	Sun

Time Sheet Template

Weekly Time Sheet   Week of: _____

Please total your hours (daily and weekly) as well as tips after your last shift of the week. Thank you.

Name:

Day	Date	Time In	Time Out	Hours	Tips	Emp	Mgr
Mon							
Tue							
Wed							
Thu							
Fri							
Sat							
Sun							
Total							

Name:

Day	Date	Time In	Time Out	Hours	Tips	Emp	Mgr
Mon							
Tue							
Wed							
Thu							
Fri							
Sat							
Sun							
Total							

Name:

Day	Date	Time In	Time Out	Hours	Tips	Emp	Mgr
Mon							
Tue							
Wed							
Thu							
Fri							
Sat							
Sun							
Total							

Daily Log Template

Daily Log   Day & Date: _____ Open: _____ Close: _____

Weather: _____ Location: _____

Notes on Location
Parking, other vendors, retail shops, interactions with local community

Team Notes
Who worked, how did they do, trainees?

Customer Feedback
Any compliments? Complaints? Regulars?

Food Quality
Was the food coming out good? Pars correct for location?

Cleaning and Maintenance
What cleaning projects were done? Any repairs needed?

Sales
How were sales? What affected sales from the norm? Weather, street fair, special events?

Other Notes
Anything else notable happen during the shift?

Daily Checklist Template

Truck Departure

☐ Lock gate/door when you go inside

☐ Turn off freezer and lowboys (circuit breaker)

☐ Unplug shoreline from truck exterior

☐ Roll up extension cord and leave in truck depot

☐ Check everything is stowed away

☐ Check for smallwares

☐ Check pars of paper from order sheet

☐ Check freshness of sides

☐ Check if you need change for drawer

☐ Check water level (must be > 50%)

☐ Check propane (must be full)

☐ Secure all drawers, cabinets, and register

☐ Check gas tank level (must be > 50%)

☐ Check mirrors

☐ Warm up engine → turn on ignition

Depot—Prep for Load:

☐ Complete order from order sheet and initial

☐ Prep required food

☐ Check smallwares are loaded

☐ Check paper is loaded

☐ Have everything ready to go downstairs

☐ Get ice

☐ Do not set anything on sidewalk

☐ Leave commissary cleaner than you found it

☐ Check menu board

On-Site Opening Checklist

☐ Check on legality of spot

☐ Check window opens

☐ Pay meter and set timer for parking period

☐ Greet other vendors, shops, and cops

☐ Stow all personal belongings overhead

☐ Turn on generator

☐ Turn on music

☐ Open canopy

Cashier—Prep for Service:

☐ Count and record drawer

☐ Get change if necessary from local bank

☐ Prep food

☐ Fill out daily log with location and weather

☐ Fill utensil drawer

☐ Check cleanliness of truck exterior

☐ Sweep and pick up trash around truck

Service

☐ Canopy open and music on

☐ Double check pars of food

☐ Be a customer: look at truck as customer

☐ Quick health inspection check

☐ Badges showing, hats, food storage, temp

Cashier—Steps of Service:

☐ Smile! Make eye contact with customers

☐ Up-sell: "Would you like a drink with that?"

☐ Give customer their receipt

☐ Say "Thank you!"

☐ Know comp and refund policies

Line—Steps of Service:

☐ Work clean

☐ Manage pars to expected volume of location

☐ FIFO

☐ Continuously clean

Cleaning Projects while in Service

☐ Wipe down ceiling and vents

☐ Wipe down cabin area

☐ Clean truck exterior (everyday)

☐ Clean windows (inside and outside)

☐ Clean register

End of Service

- ☐ Close canopy
- ☐ Record time you leave on manager log
- ☐ Check around truck for trash

Line—Close

- ☐ Turn off all equipment
- ☐ Store opened food
- ☐ Clean kitchen equipment inside and out

Cashier—Close

- ☐ Count out drawer
- ☐ Print out sales from register
- ☐ Complete all paperwork
- ☐ Daily log filled out
- ☐ Make restock list

Daily Closing Tasks

- ☐ Wipe down all surfaces (all corners and edges)
- ☐ Wipe down all cubbies (trash, hat, etc.)
- ☐ Wipe down stainless steel and all metallic surfaces
- ☐ Clean sink
- ☐ Wipe down window, ice cover, and utensil cover
- ☐ Clean gloves

Departure from Site Checklist

- ☐ Close vents/lock back door
- ☐ Close and lock all cabinets before driving
- ☐ Lock register in place
- ☐ Sweep floor or mop if super dirty
- ☐ Turn off iPod, and plug it in to charge!
- ☐ Put all loose items on floor

Return to Commissary

- ☐ Bring in trash
- ☐ Bring in perishables
- ☐ Label perishables by date and store
- ☐ Wash all dirty smallwares
- ☐ Restock truck to pars
- ☐ Put deposit in safe
- ☐ Leave commissary cleaner than you found it
- ☐ Lockdown truck: cabinets closed, loose items on floor
- ☐ Refuel on way to depot if necessary
- ☐ Drain wastewater
- ☐ Refill truck with water if necessary
- ☐ Plug in shoreline (with everything turned off)
- ☐ Check everything is stowed away
- ☐ Leave notes/new paperwork for next shift
- ☐ Check that there are no rags around on floor, etc.
- ☐ Check for random trash, drinks, etc.
- ☐ Clock out
- ☐ Lock gate on the way out

Weekly Cleaning Checklist

Monday	Deep clean cab
Tuesday	Deep clean floor
Wednesday	Deep clean cooking equipment
Thursday	Deep clean coolers and freezers
Friday	Deep clean inside of all cabinets and drawers
Saturday	Go to car wash, detail clean exterior
Sunday	Recheck all inventory is in correct spots

Maintenance Log Template

Truck Maintenance List

Truck Name: _____

Item	Problem Logged			Vendor Contacted			Repair Complete		
	Description	Date	Initial	Vendor	Date	Initial	Repair	Date	Initial

Location Journal

Map (please mark street names, ideal locations, hydrants, vendors, stores)

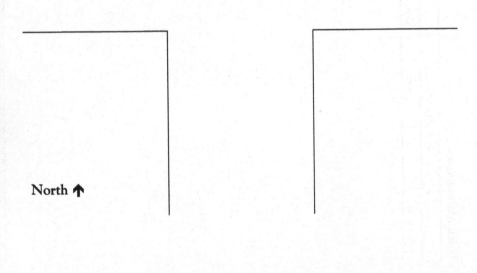

North ↑

Best Vending Locations (mark areas NOT to park with an "X"):

1. _____
2. _____
3. _____

Closest Bathroom: _____

Closest Bank: _____

Other Vendors in Neighborhood (located by letter on map)

Cart/Truck	Contact Name	Contact Phone	Days at Spot	History
A				
B				
C				

Store	Contact Name	Contact Phone	History
F			
G			
H			

Police　　　Local Precinct:_____　　Contact:_____

Date: _____

Officer Name: _____

Details of Incident: _____

_____

_____

History of Spot

Date: _____

Party Involved: _____

Details of Incident: _____

_____

_____

Appendix B
Food Truck Regulations, by City

FOLLOWING ARE SNAPSHOTS of the regulatory frameworks and food truck landscapes in several markets across the United States, organized alphabetically by the city name. Each provides a general description of rules and regulations that need to be followed by a food truck operator. Before opening a business, be sure to read up on the local rules of your municipality thoroughly so that you are aware of the latest details and developments, as regulations change quickly.

Austin, Texas

www.ci.austin.tx.us
  foodtrailersaustin.com

Overview

Austin has an active and thriving mobile food scene. Most vendors operate out of trailers in fixed locations or lots around the city. Mobile food vendors in Central Texas have united under the banner of the Food Trailer Alliance, established in May 2011 with the goal to "work together for the betterment of the industry." The mobile food scene in Austin is experiencing tremendous growth, so it's a good thing that they're organized: by the end of 2011 there were approximately 1,620 vendors.

Regulations and Permits

In order to operate, you'll need a mobile food vending operating permit for your truck, which costs from $185 to $335, and a fire department permit. At least one member of your team (probably you) will need to obtain a food manager's certification from the Austin Health Department ($110).

All mobile food units are required to operate out of a commissary. You're required to have a signed affidavit with the kitchen and keep a monthly log of visits. Because the industry is growing so quickly and there are few commissary kitchens, there is fierce competition. Without a commissary, your business will not be granted a permit. To get around the commissary constraints, many mobile food units align themselves with, and operate out of, local restaurants.

Permits differentiate between mobile units selling restricted menus of only prepackaged foods and units selling unrestricted menus of food prepared on the mobile unit. In order to get a permit for an unrestricted menu, you need to have the following installed in your truck or trailer: a triple sink and a hand sink, surfaces that can be sanitized, refrigeration, equipment to keep hot food above 135°F, thermometers, a pressurized water system and hot water heater, and the capacity to hold 15 percent more gray water than freshwater. In addition, you're required to provide restrooms for your customers and employees. When you apply for a permit, you must have a written agreement to that effect with a business within 50 feet of your trailer or a signed contract from a portable toilet supplier.

Parking

There are some roving food trucks in Austin, but most of the street food is served from trailers. Parking spots can cost up to $1,500 per month. Often trailers in the same location share overhead costs and form "trailer park eateries." Trailers must be in commercial or industrial zones but not in neighborhood office, limited office, and general office zones. They must be 50 feet away from any residential building and 20 feet away from any restaurant. Some neighborhoods have additional restrictions. The Right of Way Management Approval Network puts even more regulations on carts that sell food on the sidewalk, so food carts are the least popular type of mobile food unit in Austin.

Boston, Massachusetts

cityofboston.gov/business/mobile
   bostonmobilefood.com

Overview

Boston's city website touts food trucks as an exciting part of their local economy. The city's support of the industry is manifest in the brevity of their application process, which requires very few forms. Boston is eager to cultivate the food truck community and seems ready to make laws that create a balance between trucks and city space. Food trucks are assigned specific locations as part of the permit process. The city of Boston actually maintains a website that shows the schedule for all the trucks in the city: cityofboston.gov/business/mobile/schedule-tabs.asp.

Regulations and Permits

In order to get started, you'll need a Inspectional Services Department Health Permit signed by a health inspector get the process rolling. For vehicle inspection, prospective food truck owners must submit a sample food menu, evidence that they have a commissary, and proof that they are certified in food protection. A Use of Premise Permit, a completed Health Permit Application, and a Health Permit Fee must also be given for the application to be considered.

For new trucks, you'll need to submit a plan of the equipment and specifications of the proposed truck. You are also required to submit a completed Health Permit Application and a Health Permit fee of $100. A Massachusetts Hawkers and Peddlers License must also be obtained, along with a GPS system that must be approved and installed onboard the truck.

Parking

Once trucks are ready for the road, Boston has designated how trucks will be parked, based on assigned public and private spots. Like San Francisco, Boston makes parking a permit issue. For public vending, a vendor must have a site license. To serve on private property, you must have a copy of lease or letter of agreement with the owner of the property, a copy of the Use of Premise Permit that goes with the property, and a photo of the site where you are planning to serve.

Chicago, Illinois

cityofchicago.org

Overview

While Chicago has a vibrant food culture and great spaces to vend, the food truck industry is sorely hampered by the regulatory environment. Chicago has some of the strictest rules for food trucks in a major city, in terms of both food truck operations and parking. The biggest obstacle for vendors in Chicago is that they are not allowed to prepare food on trucks.

Regulations and Permits

One of Chicago's earliest gourmet trucks, Chicago All Fired Up, was able to get their barbecue truck licensed as a restaurant and can roll through the city, preparing food as they go. This truck remains the exception, however, and regulations for obtaining a license and managing a truck in Chicago still apply to all other trucks.

Matt Maroni of the Gaztro-Wagon introduced an ordinance to the city in 2010 to loosen regulations. Some of his major suggestions include allowing food preparation on trucks, easing the length of stay in a specific parking spot, and establishing a 100-foot courtesy distance between food trucks and traditional restaurants. The ordinance has made little headway with opponents balking at the idea of food trucks being allowed to cook onboard, even as more food trucks enter Chicago's mobile food vending scene.

In order to run a truck in Chicago, a mobile vending license can be purchased for $275 and must be displayed on the truck where it is visible to the public. Truck cleanliness must be consistent, and there must be a separation between the area on the truck where food is handled and the driver's compartment. The health department must also be notified where the vehicle is stored and cleaned.

All food must be assembled at a commissary and prepackaged for sale on the street. A separate permit for the commissary is also required. This can be either a wholesale license, which costs $660, or a retail food establishment license, which runs between $660 and $1,100. The second license is more traditional, requiring an overall inspection, the submission of plans and drawings of the space, proper storage of food and drink, and regular visits from the city's health inspector.

Parking

Parking for mobile vendors in Chicago is especially difficult. Even with growing popularity, Chicago's government has made few moves to accommodate food trucks or to improve the situation for food truck parking. Lumped in with all commercial truck parking in Chicago, mobile vendors can only stay in a parking spot for two hours and cannot sell anything after 10 PM. The city council maintains the authority to ban food trucks from vending in certain areas.

Cleveland, Ohio

city.cleveland.oh.us

Overview

After a six-month trial, the City Council of Cleveland voted in November 2011 to permanently allow mobile food vendors to park and serve customers on city streets. The new law affirms food trucks' right to exist while also setting up stricter guidelines for vending on the streets. There are currently 20 trucks licensed to operate in Cleveland, and the number is likely to grow. With a relatively receptive city government and an excited public, starting a truck in Cleveland is easier than in many other major cities.

Regulations and Permits

To start the process of getting a food truck rolling in Cleveland, you need to submit the Mobile Food Service Operation Application to the health department. The application will cover the operator's plans for the truck, down to the most basic details. The truck operator needs to provide drawn out plans that explain where everything will be on the truck. Lighting, counters, windows, entrances, and cooking equipment need to be listed, along with where hot water, freshwater, and wastewater tanks will be located. The truck must also provide a complete menu of what will be served on the truck. Food cannot be prepared or stored in a truck operator's home; it has to be prepared either on the truck or in a commercially licensed facility. The health department may place limits or conditions on the types of food sold on a truck, and if dissatisfied by the plan, may reject it. Applicants that have had their plans rejected resubmit the application with changes.

Parking

The new law allowing food trucks in Cleveland has several specific requirements. Trucks are limited to specific vending areas in the city, with popular areas including the downtown and areas around Cleveland State University open to food trucks. These areas are divided into three types: public sidewalks, public streets, and private property. Truck owners must pay $100 for a permit from the Division of Assessments and Licenses, who will assign a specific spot for the truck to operate. Cleveland trucks need to be licensed in the health district in which they are based, so licensing is essential. Every truck must own a general liability insurance policy of $100,000. Truck managers are required to purchase and wear a $60 identification badge while serving onboard the truck.

Denver, Colorado

denvergov.org

Overview

Denver has an increasingly popular varied street food scene comprised mostly of food trucks. Denver has plenty of spaces to vend and a culture that embraces the outdoors, so customers aren't afraid to go out for lunch, even in the cold. Many of the trucks are owned or operated by restaurants, which helps with the development with a fair regulatory environment to promote the industry.

Regulations and Permits

The city laws are consolidated in the Denver Food Truck Guide, issued by the City and County of Denver, and are fairly easy to understand. Denver's street food rules hadn't been revised since 1998, but as of fall 2011, the city is revisiting them in an attempt to streamline the process for food truck owners.

To start a food truck business in Denver, you need both a truck and a commissary where food will be stored and prepared. Then, you will need to schedule a licensing inspection with the Department of Environmental Health. If your truck uses propane, you will need to be inspected by the fire marshall as well. You also need to decide where you will store your truck after hours and obtain a zoning permit.

The next step is to get a business license for "Retail Food Establishments, Restaurant Mobile." You can apply in person at Excise and License. You should bring the following things with you: Affidavit of Commissary form, licensing inspection paperwork, fire inspection paperwork, zoning use permit for where vehicle will be stored, valid Colorado identification, general business questionnaire, $200 application fee, and $125 license fee. The $125 license fee is assessed annually. Once you have a license, you will be ready to start selling your food.

Parking

Vending from public streets is permitted in Denver as long as you follow all posted parking rules. The following restrictions apply: you may not sell food within 20 feet of an intersection; you may not sell food in the central business district (see Denver Food Truck Guide for a map); you may not sell food to anyone standing in the street; you may not double-park; you may not place anything in the street or on the sidewalk. This includes tables, chairs, and signs. In addition, if selling ice cream accounts for more than 10 percent of your truck's gross income, you cannot sell food on any arterial street, collector street, or laned highway.

Selling food near parks is more complicated. If you want to set up shop within 300 feet of a public park or parkway, you need a Temporary Vending Permit from the Department of Parks and Recreation. They are expensive: $100 per day or $200 per month. To apply, you will need to fill out an application form, pay $25, and submit a signed "Request for Certificate of Taxes Due," a copy of your current Business Sales License, a copy of your vehicle's insurance information, and proof of general liability insurance coverage of at least $1,000,000. You'll also need to submit your complete menu and a photograph of your truck.

If you want to sell food on private property, you will need a zoning permit from Development Services unless you plan to move your truck every 30 minutes. The type of permit you will need to get is "Retail Food Establishment, Mobile," and these cost $50 per year. Food trucks are not allowed in residential districts, but they are allowed in most downtown districts. See the Denver Food Truck Guide for geographic specifics. Food trucks may only operate on private property between 8 AM and 9 PM, and they may not operate in any single block for more than four hours per day. In addition, food trucks must be on different blocks at least 200 feet from one another and at least 200 feet from any eating and drinking establishment. They are prohibited on undeveloped, unpaved lots. They must be at least 50 feet away from residential areas. Because of these rules, most Denver food trucks operate from public parking spaces.

Los Angeles, California

lacity.org
    socalmfva.com

Overview

Los Angeles is at the heart of the food truck boom. Currently, there are about 230 gourmet food trucks in Los Angeles. Los Angeles has a street food culture that has been developed by the traditional taco trucks, so customers are used to getting meals on the street. Also, there is a lot of infrastructure to support food truck vending. Five of the largest food truck and catering truck manufacturers are nearby, and there are many commissaries to choose from. There isn't a limit on the number of permits, so there are very few barriers to entry. The fact that the weather is amazing all year-round doesn't hurt either.

Regulations and Permits

Following a change in regulations approved by the Los Angeles County Board of Supervisors, trucks are now required to have a letter grade, just like restaurants. Although trucks in Los Angeles were already getting health inspections, this is more proof that food trucks have entered the mainstream in Los Angeles.

Every food truck in Los Angeles County needs a support facility, in the form of a commissary, a mobile support unit, or some other approved facility. In Los Angeles, a commissary can serve as a storage facility for food and food serving supplies, where food is either prepared or prepackaged to be sold on a truck, where waste is disposed, and where clean water is loaded onto the truck. Truck operators must have a written and signed statement by the commissary owner that the truck is kept at that facility. Neither the truck itself nor any of the food it serves can be stored at home.

There are actually more food trucks than operators in LA, so it is relatively easy to rent a food truck. If you want to build a truck, you must submit two sets of plans of the food truck to the Vehicle Inspection Plan Check Program and a fee that covers the check and the construction evaluation. The food truck construction code is very rigorous. If you are building a truck (or buying a used truck from another state), you need to be sure your truck meets Cal Code standards, has NSF-approved equipment, and has an Ansul fire system. Once the plans have been approved and the completed truck has been inspected, a public health permit and a current certification decal will be given to the truck. In addition to these permits, the appropriate business licenses must be acquired from either City Hall or the County Business License Office.

Once trucks are set for the road, they must abide by a strict set of rules, both in terms of sanitation and parking. In terms of the Public Health Department, all raw ingredients need to be prepared in advance at the commissary. Food must be cooked to order, rather than just reheated on the truck. There must be at least one person who has been through the Food Safety Certification program onboard at all times. Menu information must be shared with the Public Health Department and include a listing of all food, condiments, and beverages that will be sold to the public.

Offenses that are actually listed by Los Angeles County are almost entirely sanitation related. A truck's health permit can be suspended or revoked if the truck lacks potable water for washing hands or utensils, if food onboard has been obtained from unauthorized sources, if food has been kept at unsafe temperatures, if general unsanitary conditions are present on the truck, if food is left unprotected, if there is no hot and cold water on the truck, and even if workers lack proper access to a bathroom.

Parking

In terms of parking, regulations are not nearly as strict as the health code. In Los Angeles, trucks are allowed to park on all public streets. However, food trucks are required to be 50 feet apart when street vending. The major challenge to parking is a requirement to be within 200 feet of a bathroom for employees. There is no permit process, so most trucks end up paying not only for the meter but also, once their allotted time has run out, paying a ticket, usually at around $50.

Miami, Florida

miamigov.com

Overview

Food trucks are very popular in Miami. While the concept of street food is relatively new, it has been wholeheartedly embraced by the local community. So far, regulation of food trucks is relatively relaxed. The best thing about Miami is the weather. It is beautiful all year-round, and there lots of outdoor festivals, which are great vending opportunities.

Regulations and Permits

To vend in Miami, you can operate one of three ways: with a peddler's license, a temporary use/special event permit, or a temporary use of vacant space. A peddler's license allows you to vend like an ice cream vendor, where you are constantly on the move. Using social media to establish and keep lines long will be important, as will a line that can be quickly set up and shut down. A temporary use/special event permit allows you to vend on private property or public property. You can vend on private property a maximum of two times per year for as long as two weeks each, for a total of four weeks. On public property, you can vend a maximum of 10 times per year for as long as two weeks each, for a total of 20 weeks. Finally, with a temporary use of vacant land permit, you can vend on vacant land for six months. These permits can be extended for as long as two years in six-month increments. However, to obtain a vacant land permit, the property must truly be vacant. Parking lots and abandoned properties do not qualify as vacant properties. The property must be clearly owned but not have any active use.

Parking

If you're operating as a peddler, your truck must constantly be on the move. With a temporary use permit, you can park on public, private, or vacant property.

Milwaukee, Wisconsin

city.milwaukee.gov

Overview

Food trucks are a recent phenomenon in Milwaukee, which began with the opening of Streetza Pizza in 2009. Since then, trucks have been booming in Milwaukee, and it is still relatively easy to acquire the necessary permits to run a truck in this Wisconsin metropolis.

Regulations and Permits

To operate in Milwaukee and to sell more than just prepackaged food, food trucks need a food peddler's license. If you are selling meals from your truck, you will also need a food dealer's license and an occupancy permit under your business name, along with a notarized statement allowing you to utilize someone else's kitchen.

Besides permits, every truck in Milwaukee needs a so-called service base, where there is room for servicing, cleaning, inspecting, and maintening the truck. Private homes cannot be used for service bases. The service facility needs a four-compartment stainless steel sink with drainboards for utensil washing. There must be a sink for hand washing and a sink with a threaded tap so that the truck's water tank can be filled from a food-grade water hose. There also needs to be a mop sink or waste drain for getting rid of wastewater. Room for food and supplies must be available in the service base. The building must also be up to Wisconsin codes concerning floors, wall finishes, equipment, and lighting. The schedule of your truck must also be posted at all times.

If you are already operating a permanent licensed establishment, it can potentially be used as a service base for your truck. If the facility is being shared or leased with another party, the Milwaukee Health Department will inspect it and license the location in your name. A written agreement between you and the owner of the facility is necessary. A truck doesn't need to have a service base if it is proved to inspectors that the truck can operate and remain up to code without the facilities of a service base.

On the truck itself, there must be a pressurized hand-wash sink with hot and cold water. If you are processing food, you will need utensil sinks with pressurized hot and cold water. There must be enough water on your truck to keep sinks ready at all times while away from your service base. In addition to a larger sink, trucks where food is being prepared need a water tank that has at least 40 gallons of storage. The truck's wastewater tank must be 15 percent larger than the truck's water tank. There also must be a partition between the driver's compartment of the truck and the space where food is being prepared.

Parking

Food trucks cannot park or sell within 300 feet of an entrance to a school while it is in session. Trucks can park on residential blocks for only two hours. These parking periods must be broken up with six-hour breaks. On a nonresidential public street block, trucks can park for only one hour per day, unless they are in compliance with all local parking time limits and regulations. Vendors are also barred from selling food or merchandise two hours before and one hour after any scheduled event within 500 feet of several Milwaukee event spaces, including the Midwest Express Center and the Milwaukee Public Museum. Food trucks cannot block entry to any business or residence. There must also be a minimum 5-foot clearance on sidewalks for pedestrians.

Food can only be sold between the hours of 9 PM and 6 AM if your truck has a nighttime operation permit. This does not apply during special occasions, including the Fourth of July and Memorial Day.

New York, New York

nyc.gov
   nycfoodtrucks.org

Overview

Street vending has been an important part of the history and culture of New York City since the 1600s. Today, the vast majority of street vendors are food carts selling hot dogs, nuts, coffee, halal food, or soft-serve ice cream trucks. Since 2007, there has been an explosion of differentiated branded street food on the streets of New York. Vending in New York is extremely difficult because of the scarcity of parking, a recent interpretation of a law on the books since 1965 that makes it illegal to vend from metered parking, rigorous requirements for mobile food-vending licenses for the people who work on trucks and carts, and a cap on the number of permits for street-vending units (be they carts or trucks.)

Regulations and Permits

In New York City, a mobile food-vending license refers to the certification of a person. A mobile food-vending permit refers to the certification on a vehicle. In order to vend, you will need both a licensed operator and a permitted vehicle or cart.

The process to obtain a mobile food vendor license is quite lengthy. The quickest you might be able to obtain a license is in six to eight weeks. One challenge is that each applicant needs to provide a New York State Certificate of Authority to Collect Sales Tax. This may be easy for you as the owner of the business, but it is quite a slow process to obtain a Certificate of Authority to Collect Sales Tax for each employee. Even once you have completed the paperwork and been approved, you need to wait for the actual permit to come in the mail. Currently, mobile food vendors are only allowed to work when their license is upon their person. The fines for vending without a license start at $1,000, which is very high, given the industry.

The same permit is used for carts or for food trucks. Even though there is one permit that is used on both carts and trucks, there are different construction requirements for each of the two types of mobile food-vending units. There isn't a cap on the total number of permits, but there is a cap on the total number of street vending permits. NYC Code allows for 3,000 year-round, citywide, mobile food street-vending permits, and 1,000 seasonal citywide mobile food street vending permits, which are valid from April to October. There are an additional 250 borough-specific food- and street-vending permits, of which there are 50 per borough. NYC Parks Department has authority over all vending in NYC Parks. A NYC citywide mobile food-vending permit isn't valid in a park or on any streets adjacent to or abutting a park.

Because NYC street vending permits are renewable and all the permits have been allocated, there is a very long waiting list (which is closed for new applicants). The best way to get into vending in New York City is by obtaining a restricted area permit. Restricted area permits allow the use of a food truck or food cart in one specific location. The primary requirement of a restricted area permit is a contract with the owner of the lot or property where you will vend. Because open space is scarce in New York City, restricted area permits are generally used by the Parks Department to permit mobile food units in NYC Parks (nycgovparks.org).

For mobile food vendors that are participating in a special event, it is possible to get permitted as a temporary food service establishment.

Parking

Food trucks with a street permit can vend on NYC streets, aside from a list of approximately 120 restricted streets (nyc.gov/html/doh/

downloads/pdf/permit/mfv_restricted_streets.pdf). However, they must follow all the parking requirements for regular vehicles in addition to a number of requirements specific to food trucks. Mobile food trucks may not vend within 10 feet of subway entrance, 10 feet of crosswalks, 20 feet of a store entrance, 20 feet of another street vendor (cart or truck), 25 feet of corner of curb, 200 feet of any public or private school, or 500 feet of public market. Furthermore, food trucks may not block pedestrians so as to significantly impede traffic, and as discussed earlier, food trucks may not vend in a park without a special permit.

In 2011, it became illegal to vend from metered parking spaces. According to NYC Code: Title 34 §4-08(h)(8) "No peddler, vendor, hawker, or huckster shall park a vehicle at a metered parking space for purposes of displaying, selling, storing, or offering merchandise for sale from the vehicle." While I personally believe street food prepared to order is a service, the New York State Supreme Court ruled on February 25, 2011, that street food constitutes merchandise. After an initial appeal of the ruling was dismissed on May 25, 2011, NYC Agencies have started enforcing the no-vending-from-metered-parking rules. Since that time, food truck operators have reported revenues of 30 to 70 percent of their previous sales, and several food trucks have gone out of business.

Philadelphia, Pennsylvania

business.phila.gov
   facebook.com/phillymfa

Overview

Street food in Philly has long been a popular and accepted part of the food industry, and the city has a fast-developing food truck industry.

Regulations and Permits

Philadelphia allows trucks, trailers, pushcarts, and stands. There is no cap on the number of licenses. Permits are renewable annually, subject to good inspection results. Permits are tied to specific locations. As part of the application process, you'll need to apply to vend in a specific area. A committee reviews the applications and will either approve or deny your application based on a number of criteria, including the vending density in that neighborhood.

In order to apply for a permit, you'll need to submit the plans for your truck and commissary via the same plan review that a restaurant would use to apply for a permit. Like restaurants, all employees are subject to Food Establishment Personnel Food Safety Certification requirements.

As of 2010, Philadelphia placed no restrictions on durations of vendor stops. Vendors are required to operate from a commissary. You still need to have your truck to pass inspection before applying for your permit, but zoning no longer applies to nonpermanent retail businesses (apart from the prohibited streets mentioned earlier).

Parking

Most food trucks in Philly tend to vend in stable locations. Food trucks pay $3,000 per year for a "legal" spot on public property (there were only 400 in the city as of 2010). There is an active community of food trucks vending on private property as well, notably on the UPenn campus.

Portland, Oregon

portlandonline.com

Overview

Portland has an extremely active food cart scene that has been embraced by city regulators as a way to incubate small businesses, create jobs, and activate the streetscape. Most mobile food businesses are run as carts that vend at lots.

Regulations and Permits

Mobile food units are regulated as vehicles in Oregon. They must not be longer than 16 feet, and they must not require a special permit to be moved. The unit must have wheels and must not be permanently connected to any utilities.

Mobile food units in Portland are divided into four categories. Class I units serve only prepackaged food and nonperishable beverages. Class II units can have a hot or cold holding display for unpackaged foods, but they may not cook or assemble food in the unit. Class III units can cook and assemble anything but raw meat. Class IV units have no menu restrictions. Any unit serving unpackaged foods must have hand-washing facilities. All types of units are required to provide bathrooms to their customers, either by parking close to a public restroom or having an agreement with a local business. Units may provide seating to their customers only if the restroom is a quarter-mile away or closer.

Mobile food units need to have a commissary, unless they meet all of the following criteria: equipment is onboard to keep food colder than 41°F or hotter than 140°F, employees can wash their hands in warm water, all dishes can be washed in hot water and then stored inside the unit, and the unit contains both freshwater and wastewater, and the waste-water can be disposed of via an approved sewage system. Units that sell only prepackaged foods can list warehouses as their commissaries.

Before you open a food cart, you must submit blueprints and menus to a plan review specialist. This costs $290. Once your plan is approved, you may start construction on your unit. You will need to check to see if you need approval from other agencies, such as the fire marshal. Then, before you open for business, you will need to submit a mobile food unit license application. A one-year license costs $340. After your preopening health inspection, you will finally be ready to start selling food.

All mobile food unit employees must have a food handler's card. You can pay $10, take an easy online test, and print out the card from any computer. You must comply with food safety regulations, and your unit will be subject to health inspections twice a year. You also must notify Multnomah County Environmental Health whenever your menu, route, or ownership changes.

Parking

Because there are no zoning restrictions on mobile food units parked on private property, most food carts, trucks, and trailers park in private lots. Paying for a month of parking (which costs between $300 and $600) can be cheaper than paying daily rates. Therefore, the majority of mobile food vendors in Portland chooses not to move around every day.

But the zoning regulations on mobile food businesses that use public street parking are much more strict. They can't park on the same block as any residential property for more than 10 minutes. Once they leave a block, they may not return for two hours. In addition, trucks may not be left unattended for more than 30 minutes. They must not be parked or stored overnight on any public property.

San Francisco, California

sfgov.org
   sfdph.org/dph/eh/Food/mobile.asp
   www.sf-planning.org/index.aspx?page=2846
   www.sfdpw.org/index.aspx?page=1376
   sfcartproject.com

Overview

San Francisco has a vibrant street food culture. As a dense urban area with an active foodie population and relatively mild weather, San Francisco is a great market for food trucks. Food truck vendors operate from stable city-approved locations. Weekly events coordinated by Off the Grid (offthegrid.com) positively highlight food trucks and connect them to the local community.

Regulations and Permits

In 2010, San Francisco's Board of Supervisors overhauled the process of starting a food truck in San Francisco. While the law does not clarify commissary standards and leaves certain issues wide open for interpretation, the law is notable in its discussion of truck parking and behavior, with few other major cities having anything that up to date.

Food truck applicants go through the Public Works Department and submit several fees to get started with their Mobile Food Facility application: a filing fee of $125, a notification fee of $200, and an inspection fee of $383 for a single location. Additional location inspections each cost $191.50. Tweaks to the truck's setup, such as any change of location, change of hours to after 8 PM, or adding a new location requires a filing fee of $85, and there is an annual renewal fee of $125.

Once the fees are covered, an application can be submitted. A mobile food facility application form will cover what's on the truck, what the truck will be serving, proposed locations where the truck will operate, a diagram of how the truck will be parked in the proposed location, and any other pertinent information.

San Francisco food trucks need to be built out to Cal Code requirements, plus a few regulatory overlays specific to San Francisco. You'll need a three-compartment sink, hand towel dispenser, and soap dispenser. All equipment must be NSF-approved and must heat or cool to the correct temp.

Once the truck has been approved, the permit, business license, Certificate of Sanitation decal, and an identification card need to be somewhere that is visible to customers. San Francisco's food truck rules are also notable in advocating that noise and smell will be kept to appropriate levels, safety will be maintained, and trash will be picked up within 100 feet of the truck following a shift. Any violation of these policies risks revocation of the permit.

Trucks can also lose their license if they commit fraud, work in unsanitary conditions, or do not utilize their permitted spot for over six months. San Francisco is notable for bringing their food truck laws up to date.

Parking

Food vendors are permitted for specific locations on public streets in San Francisco by the Department of Public Works. It is also possible to get a temporary use authorization (TUA) to vend on public or private property with permission.

Seattle, Washington

seattle.gov/economicdevelopment/mobilefood

Overview

Seattle has a great food culture and a very clean regulatory scheme for operating food trucks. At the beginning of 2012, only about 50 branded food trucks were serving the Seattle metro area, which is home to almost 3.5 million people. For those who don't mind the near-constant rain, there's room for a lot of growth in this market.

Regulations and Permits

First, you'll need to register your trade name and get a Washington state business license. This requires you to fill out one form online and pay $20. You will also need a Seattle business license. Then you need to obtain a Conversion Vendor/Medical Unit Insignia, which costs about $57, by filling out another online form and creating a plan for review and approval. If you're planning to use liquid petroleum gas and/or an open flame to prepare food, you need a permit from the Seattle Fire Marshal. It's called an Annual Liquid Propane Gas (LPG) Permit for Food Vending, and it will run you more than $300. You can't do it online, either—you'll have to call the Fire Marshal at 206-386-1450 for more information, and then apply in person or via snail mail.

The last—but perhaps most complicated—permit that you need is a Mobile Food Unit Permit from Seattle and King County Public Health. This is a major expenditure: depending on your menu and how many hours you want to operate per day, it may cost between $1,200 and $3,600. It's a three-step process. First, you need to use the Mobile Food Service Plan Guide checklist to make sure all of your documents are in order. In addition to the permits mentioned earlier, you'll need paperwork regarding your commissary kitchen, restroom agreement, routes, food preparation flow chart, menu, business operation plan, and the construction of your truck (inside and out). Once you've assembled everything on the checklist, you can submit a Mobile Plan Review Application. After this business plan is approved, you can submit your Mobile Food Service Permit Application. This third form is the shortest. You can submit it online.

Parking

There are four categories of parking spots for food trucks. You can mix and match as desired.

1. **Public right-of-way:** If you want to sell your wares from public parking spots, you will need a Street Use Permit for Curb Space Vending from Seattle Department of Transportation (SDOT). A one-year permit costs about $500 in administrative fees and then an additional $350 to $700 for each four-hour block in a week. (So if you want to park on the street from 10 AM to 2 PM on Mondays and Wednesdays, that's two blocks.) This allows you to park only in designated food vehicle zones. In early 2012, food truck businesses seemed to be concentrated in Renton and East Side and South Lake Union.

2. **Event vending:** You will need a Street Use Permit for Stadium and Event Center Vending. They are available from SDOT on a monthly or seasonal (six-month) basis. They cost a $146 administrative fee, plus $110 to $170 per month.

3. **Private property:** You can sell food from a truck on private property as long as you have the consent of the owner and an Intermittent Temporary of Permanent Use Permit. Alternatively, if you're willing to sell from a preexisting private parking lot, Portland-style, you don't need a permit at all! But you can't leave your truck there overnight.

4. **Public parks:** If you spend $75 on a Use Permit from Seattle Parks and Recreation, you can sell your food in public parks.

Washington, DC

dc.gov

    dcfoodtrucks.org

Overview

The food truck scene in Washington is very well developed. There are lots of foodies in DC to support the food truck culture and lots of great places to park. Unfortunately, the regulatory oversight is a bit antiquated. While there are proposals for more fair and equitable laws to regulate the trucks, food trucks in the District of Columbia operate under laws designed decades ago for ice cream trucks.

Regulations and Permits

Setting up a licensed food truck in DC involves several bureaucratic hurdles but is still achievable. The process begins by getting a Certified Food Protection Manager Identification from the DC Department of Health for $35. Next, you must submit a plan and a proposed menu to the Department of Health's Food Compliance for a $100 fee.

Once this has been approved, you need a blueprint of your proposed truck. This plan must be submitted to the Department of Health to ensure it will pass inspection. The only restriction on design for a DC food truck is size, with maximum dimensions at 18.5 feet long, 10.5 feet tall, and 8 feet wide.

When the truck is completed, the Department of Health will do a final inspection of the truck. If propane is being used or a deep fryer is installed, the DC Fire Marshal must also conduct an inspection. A Vending Application must also be submitted to the Department of Health with information covering the truck, contact information, and operational hours.

In addition to making sure the truck is up to code, you must also maintain a relationship with a depot or commissary. A written and signed letter concerning the depot must be submitted to the Health Department for approval.

Once the truck is up and running, it must undergo regular health inspections. Food trucks in DC undergo health inspections just like brick-and-mortar restaurants but are billed by the health department every time they are inspected.

Parking

Legally, trucks are only able to solicit customers who flag them down, since the law was originally designed for ice cream trucks. Customers can also alert the truck of where they are via social media, but once the truck has served all customers, it must leave immediately.

In December 2011, the DC Department of Public Works began issuing tickets to vendors parked for more than two hours in one location. While the DC Police maintain that the crackdown is being applied to all parking offenders, the DC Food Truck Association argues that food trucks are being targeted, while other parking offenders are ignored. In January 2012, police got even stricter, forcing trucks that didn't have a line of people waiting to move and fining them $50. Each time the truck is fined, the amount increases.

Appendix C
Social Media Guides

THIS APPENDIX LISTS the top three top social media sites and gives instructions on how to get started promoting and communicating about your food truck on Twitter, Facebook, and Foursquare.

Twitter

Twitter is a great way to build a base of followers and keep them updated on news about your truck. Since it is easily accessible on mobile devices, many food truck owners use it daily to update their locations and make it easier for people to find them. Keep in mind that tweets must be brief (140 characters or fewer).

Here are some instructions to get you started:

1. Sign up for a free account on twitter.com.
2. Get a sense of the Twitter landscape by following friends or local businesses. To do this, type their name into the search field and then select them. Consider following other trucks in your area.
3. Personalize your account by editing your profile. You can add a picture, a website, and a concise description of your truck in the "bio" section.

4. Tweet by typing a brief message in the "What's happening?" box. This is a great way to let the world know where your truck will be and when.

5. Get followers. Advertise your Twitter name via your other social media accounts, on your website, and even on your truck itself. Follow anyone who follows you.

6. Reach out especially to websites like roaminghunger.com that consolidate data about the day-to-day locations of many different food trucks. Give them your Twitter name and invite them to follow you.

7. Check the @Mentions tab to read feedback from your followers. Interact with them by hitting Reply.

Facebook

Facebook is similar to Twitter because it helps you keep your fans and your customer base updated on your business and latest news. The benefit to using Facebook is that it allows you to write longer entries, add more details about your truck and its menu, and provide a history of past conversations and news.

1. Go to www.facebook.com. Under the green "Sign Up" button, there's a link that allows you to create a page for a celebrity, band, or business. Click on this link, and follow the instructions to enter information about your food truck.

2. Once you have a page, you can click "Edit info" to add photos, menus, and more information about your business.

3. At the top of your page, there will be an option to link your Facebook page to your Twitter account. This is a good idea, because it will make it easier to update all of your social media accounts at once.

4. Find your fans by inviting your friends to "Like" your page.

5. Follow the instructions to promote your Facebook page on your website.

6. Post status updates. If you get tired of just posting when and where your truck will be, consider making your page more interactive by posting discussion questions such as, "We are adding a vegan

dumpling on our menu. What should we call it?" You can also post relevant and related news within the industry.

Foursquare

Foursquare allows people to use their smartphones to "check in" at various locations. It is another way to help your customers track you down, and it helps you set up special offers that reward your most loyal fans and followers. For example, the person who checks in most often at any location is awarded "mayorship" at that place. If you give your mayor special discounts, customers may compete to see who can check in most frequently.

The following lists the 11 steps to getting started in Foursquare.

1. Go to www.foursquare.com, and click "Join Now."
2. Follow the instructions, and use your Facebook account to sign up.
3. Expand your circle by adding your Facebook friends to your Foursquare account.
4. Add Twitter to your Foursquare account.
5. Search for your food truck on Foursquare—it's possible that someone else has already added it. If so, follow the instructions to claim your business.
6. If you don't see your food truck on Foursquare already, scroll to the bottom of the search results and click on "Add a new venue to Foursquare."
7. Enter your food truck's information. In the address field, type "Moving Target!" On the map, try to choose your truck's most frequent location.
8. Use your mobile phone to check in to your food truck as often as possible. This will help other Foursquare users track your truck's location. If you have drivers and other employees, make checking in on Foursquare a daily duty for them.
9. When you claim your venue, a window cling will be sent to you. Put it in your truck so that your customers will know that they can check in.
10. Incentivize your customers to check in by adding specials. Once you've claimed your venue, click on "Manager Tools," then

"Campaigns," then "Start a Campaign," then "Add a Special." Select a type of special, and then specify the reward that you are offering to your customers.

11. Foursquare recommends that moving target venues set up a Check-in Special that is awarded to their customers the first time they check in. This helps them keep track of your customers and award points and mayorships. Follow the instructions above, and select "Check-in Special" to set this feature up.

Appendix D
Interviews with Food Truck Entrepreneurs

Interview 7: Alex Rein of Kelvin Natural Slush Co.

Kelvin Natural Slush Co. sells all natural frozen slush beverages. They have reinvented an American classic, with unique and sophisticated flavors like spicy ginger, tangy citrus, and green tea that are mixed with swirls of all natural, pureed fruit and chopped herbs, like basil or mint. Kelvin Natural Slush Co. won the Vendy Award for best dessert in 2010. They have also been listed as one of America's top 20 food trucks by *QSR* magazine and one of America's top 15 street food vendors by Relish.com.

Q: How do you communicate with customers?

We're big into social media, and we really make an effort to connect with customers and get feedback from them. We use Facebook to post things that either interest us or are about us, such as when we won the Vendy, [an annual award and competition organized by the Street

(continued)

(*continued*)

Vendor Project] in 2010. Twitter is the most important thing we do, and is our best means of talking to people.

Q: Did you find you had a lot of problems after the Midtown ban?

A lot of the food trucks depend on the midtown business lunch rush. We actually don't because we're more of a dessert, late afternoon snack. We do better later in the afternoon and in areas where people are milling around—going to the park or doing some shopping. But we were asked to move a couple of times as a result of the crackdown. It's not just losing a spot that's a problem, it's losing the time it takes to find a new spot, update where you are, relocate, and set up again.

We're getting a cart for 6th Street and Bleecker and are working to have a permit for a set spot. We'll know we'll be there every day, and that takes some of the issues out of mobile vending. Right now we're looking to expanding in that direction, more secure spots.

Q: What is the best thing that you have on your truck that sets you apart from other trucks?

Slushies are pretty much all we sell. In the summer, we do carry some retail items like brownies, chocolate bars, and potato chips, but our primary business is slush. We have two flavors, ginger citrus and tea, and those can be customized with your choice of natural mixes, pureed fruit, chopped mint, chopped basil, Pomegranate teas—pretty much anything we think would mix in nicely. Some of the fruits we offer are white peach, raspberry, strawberry, mango. Our beverages are all natural and no high-fructose corn syrup. We put a high priority on cleanliness, and we wash our machines every day.

Q: What has been your experience with parking?

At this point we do have several spots that are our go-to spots where [people and local businesses] have gotten to know us. In terms of other vendors around us, we try to be as respectful as possible. Because our product is a drink and more of a treat, we don't directly compete with a lot of the other trucks, so people are pretty open to having us park near them, whether it's Rickshaw, Korilla, or Taïm.

Q: What are the best and worst qualities of street vending for you?

The high point is that we generally have a lot of fun. Obviously you take the business part very seriously, but it's meant to be fun—it's a slushie. It's a fun experience, everyone's in a good mood and excited to get the product. I really enjoy interacting with the customers and talking to people. I think the response we've had has been overwhelmingly positive from our customers, and I think we're becoming something more. Our first year, we won the best dessert Vendy, a high point. Seeing a business grow and seeing the response we've gotten has been great.

Q: How did your background as a lawyer play into selling slushies?

A little bit; not what I did in my day-to-day job. It helped though with negotiating contracts, the focus on branding, and the attention to detail in terms of getting the business off the ground. When I was practicing, I did commercial real estate finance, and there were a lot of contracts. Not a lot of direct carryover, but getting our own contracts, getting a trademark all came from those experiences. It helps to navigate that world, working through red tape, dealing with the government, and dealing with the city. There are a lot of things that come up that my background was useful for.

Q: How much did you consider branding while setting up your truck?

Short answer: a lot. We wanted to distinguish ourselves. We wanted a strong name so that it would be distinctive and that people would recognize us. We have uniforms with the logo, branded cups with our name, and the vinyl wrap of the truck. We paid a lot of attention to the design and tone of our website, Facebook page, Twitter account, and made sure that everything portrayed us as a premium brand because ultimately what we're offering is a high-end slushie.

Q: What do you look for in your employees?

We want upbeat. We have a fun product, and we want people to have a good experience. We want everyone who visits the truck to have a good

(continued)

(continued)

experience, so we really hammer that home: be friendly, smile, give recommendations, as many samples as anyone wants.

Q: How do you deal with customer complaints?

It depends on the type of complaint. If the complaint is in an e-mail or a tweet or a Twitter direct message, we try to address it directly with whoever complained, apologize, and, depending on how serious the complaint is, offer to buy them a slush if they'll come back. We really try to engage and discuss the problem with customers and then try to handle the issue with our staff.

Q: What advice would you give yourself looking back?

I wish I had known about employee licensing and parking regulations. Licensing was one of the toughest challenges of our first year.

I was on the truck literally every day. I drove it into the city, closed, cleaned it, drove it back. This was in our first year, and we didn't know exactly when we were going to open, and it was hard to hire people since we couldn't know what our hours were going to be, and I wasn't sure what it would be like to get the system up and running. Someone starting out will have to expect to work hard, and you have to be prepared to adapt and deal with unperceived challenges.

Q: What advice would you give those starting a food truck?

Work very, very long hours. The perception is that it's easier than starting a brick-and-mortar restaurant, and in some respects it is, but you're not going to be successful just because it's a food truck. You need to focus on all the things you would focus on in a regular restaurant setting, along with truck concerns. There are issues that are particular to food trucks and do creep up, and you have to be flexible, changing things on the fly, and adapting to changing circumstances. Whether it's the truck breaking down or two other trucks taking a spot you usually go to, you have to be ready. A lot of things happen on the fly.

Prepare as much as you can by talking to other truck owners or suppliers or getting a real sense of the overall business. We tried to do that as much as we could going into it, as this was my first foray into the food service industry. In our experience, people in the food truck world have been helpful, very friendly.

Interview 8: Andrew Miscioscia of Andy's Italian Ices

Andy's offers fresh Italian ices created with high quality ingredients in individual handmade batches. The most striking aspect of Andy's Italian Ices is that he carries over 60 flavors on his sparkling clean truck. Andy was introduced to the hospitality business by working for one of his family's gourmet food markets. The attention-to-quality ingredients, cleanliness, and attentive service translated well into his Italian ices dessert truck.

Q: What are the best and worst parts of street vending?

The best part of street vending is the vibe of Manhattan; I love the vibe of Manhattan. Seeing all the different people, meeting different people, it's always exciting. Going from one part of Manhattan to another part of Manhattan, there's just always so many different vibes and arts and cultures.

The bad part of street vending is that it gets looked down upon in New York by some restaurants and others. Not as much with me because I'm a dessert truck, but it still aggravates people, and people don't want me to be out in front of their house or their townhome, whatever the circumstances might be, so sometimes that aggravates people as well.

Q: What was your background before the truck?

My family has been well known to own grocery stores in the past. After my father passed away, I took over one of his grocery stores at age 17, so I was thrown into the business pretty quickly. Over the years, I've learned so much about the grocery business, about the food industry, the PR side of things, thinking outside of the box to get people to the store, so I had a little background in the food business. How I got specifically into Italian ices was that there was a very well-known Italian ice company in our area because I live on Long Island and not in Manhattan, and they do very, very well, and I've always looked up to their company and their franchise. So I decided with all the recipes I'd accumulated from over the 10, 12, 15 years of working at my family's grocery store, of ice cream, gelato, and ices, I decided to do my own twist-off. That's how, lo and behold, Andy's Italian Ices came to be, but I decided not to do it in a store but do it mobile.

(continued)

(continued)

Q: What do you do for branding?

I've honestly been very quiet until now. Last season was really my first season in Manhattan, it was my third year in operation with the truck. This year I actually am going to go more full blast, Twittering more, Facebooking more. I'm also going to be doing a lot more promotional things, especially for my Manhattan Facebook fans—come to the truck and taste something, or buy a small ice and get one free. We're going to have an Italian ice happy hour.

Q: How do you communicate and get the word out to customers?

I've been written up in a few magazines here on Long Island, and I got a lot of publicity from that. I do use Twitter a lot, I use Facebook a lot, I have both of my accounts linked together so that when I tweet, it goes on my Facebook, and when I Facebook, it goes on Twitter. I do a lot of cross-promotions with that, and I always try to keep the customers up to speed on where I am, where I'm going, what I'm doing, and when I'm going to be there. This season we have a whole new website, so on our actual website, it gives you a list of where we're supposed to be and when we're supposed to be there, and obviously we have the option to change that in case we have a private event book, which does happen quite often during the summer. For example, even though we're supposed to be at Astor Place at night or Union Square, I'm still able to go online and let the customers know we can't be there because we have a private event, and I always tweet and Facebook if something comes up like that.

Q: What makes your truck special?

I used a Mercedes Sprinter Truck. I figured I'd stand out a little bit more than the norms because it's a brand new truck, it's very slick looking, it's very modern looking, I'm not the typical box truck or the Mister Softee truck blowing out diesel fumes. I'm also very green on the truck. I have two alternate power sources, I have a quiet home generator that powers everything—it's the cleanest, most pure generator you can buy right now—and then I also have batteries that I work off. If

I don't want to use the generator or we're in a clean environment and I don't want to lose the kids with exhaust fumes, or whatever the circumstances may be, I can always switch over to my green power as well. But the thing that makes it stand out the most is the colors—I used a lot of vibrant colors. I try to keep the truck as clean-looking as possible. I didn't want to wrap it like some of the other trucks do. I didn't want to get all crazy with the decals like that. I tried to keep it simple clean and classy. I know it sounds a little crazy, but that's what I did on my truck, and the fact that I bought a brand new truck and I didn't buy a used box truck also makes the truck look 20 times better as well.

Q: What do you do for upkeep on the truck?

We clean the truck every single day. We serve espresso and coffee and things like that, so obviously the daily cleanings need to be done. The waste tank needs to be dumped, the freshwater needs to be filled. We blow through a lot of water on food trucks because our Italian ices are just fresh fruit, water, sugar, so it tends to get a little sticky on the truck, and it's kind of hard not to wash your hands constantly.

We are frozen foods, so we don't really have to worry about the tomatoes going bad for tomorrow or something not being ripe enough. Our biggest worry at the end of the night is just making sure that the truck is plugged in and that it has power and that we're not going to lose products for the day and that nothing melts on us.

I'm very crazy about the truck being clean on the inside and the outside. I'm a very firm believer in keeping the truck clean. You never know when a health inspector can come by. Even for people just standing outside the truck, popping their heads inside the serving window just to look, you show that you have a clean operation. It really shows a lot for your company and represents your name and your branding as well.

Q: What are your plans for the future of the truck?

I'm probably going to look to do another truck or a cart. I can't foresee the future (I wish I could!) because it would help me out in a lot of different ways right now, but I would like to see another truck in the near future.

(continued)

(continued)

Q: What do you serve on the truck?

We serve on the truck between 40 and 45 water and cream ices. All our water ices are made with fresh fruits, so we're a much healthier choice. You can actually taste the fresh mangos, the strawberries, the bananas, the watermelon in all of our ices; it's actually very pure ice. Our cream ices are actually dairy free, so if you have any allergies or are lactose intolerant, it's usually okay to have one of our cream ices because it gives you the same texture as an ice cream or a gelato but without all the guilt or bloating of dairy-like ice cream. We also have three sugar-free flavors of ice onboard in which we use royal agave for sweetener. We also serve a full line of beverages like water, sodas, ice teas, and we also have coffee, espresso, cappuccino, and hot chocolate. We use Lavazza, which is a very well-known Italian company we use for our coffee. It's a very deep espresso bean. A lot of people love us for our coffee.

Q: What advice do you have for someone wanting to start their own truck?

I don't even know where to start. Cross your i's, dot your t's, and just realize and recognize what you're getting into before you jump into it. Yes, it is a great business; yes, it is very fun, but what goes on behind the scenes, people don't get to realize until they're actually in it. Then they're hitting themselves in the head, or saying "Oh my god, I should have thought of that sooner." Even to this day, I am still modifying my truck, I have things going on right now. This is my down season, and I'm still spending money on the truck to do this, to move that, to put this in this location, to make this better for my employee, to make this better for me if I have to work the truck. God forbid, there's always going to be that if, and, or but, but it's just the nature of the business.

Interview 9: David Shapiro of Taïm Mobile

Taïm Mobile is the mobile offshoot of the extremely popular Taïm Falafel & Smoothie Bar. Taïm Mobile offers a wide menu of delicious kosher food including falafel, hummus, and smoothies.

Q: Why did you build a truck? Why did you choose a mobile operation rather than opening another store?

I used to work in finance in midtown, and I thought the food trucks circling the area were just so cool. I had no experience in the food business though, so I went looking for the right partner. I looked for either someone with a new but untested concept to start something new or for a successful restaurant looking to expand its brand. Through my friend and future partner Nektarios I was introduced to Stefan and Einat, the owners of Taïm. Right away, we knew it was a match.

Of course Einat and Stefan had always wanted another Taïm and always thought to open a second location, but the right time for that had not come yet, and at the time they were busy opening Balaboosta, their restaurant in SoHo. So in a sense, we met each other at exactly the right time. They wanted to expand the Taïm brand but were not ready for another location yet, and I was interested in opening a food truck with a restaurant partner—it all worked out perfectly.

Q: What benefits did you see from starting a truck that you didn't have at a restaurant or kiosk?

Of course the biggest difference between having a truck and a restaurant is that a food truck is mobile. The truck literally takes the brand around the city, serving our food in all neighborhoods. Also, the truck interacts and communicates with customers in a way that's nearly impossible for a restaurant or kiosk—for example, Twitter. Also, while initially we thought that the costs of running the truck would be much less than those of a fixed location, we soon found that this was not the case. The truck pays parking rent, commissary, and prep kitchen space rent, fines and parking tickets, high insurance, very high electric costs (generators), and much more maintenance costs than a fixed location.

(continued)

(continued)

Q: What were the cost differences between a truck and another form of food service?

While initially we thought that the costs of running the truck would be much less than those of a fixed location we soon found that this was not the case. The truck pays parking rent, commissary and prep kitchen space rent, fines and parking tickets, high insurance, very high electric costs (generators), and many more maintenance costs than a fixed location. Also, whenever there is an important maintenance issue to be taken care of, we have to close the business for the day. So there are even additional costs associated with that, too.

Q: What kind of mobility do trucks provide compared to other types of mobile vendors?

I guess we first have to define what mobility means. Is the more mobile vendor the one who can change locations more frequently and on shorter notice? Or is it the one who can vend from more locations (i.e., the one who is more agile/flexible?) If we use the former criterion, then food trucks take the cake. Regarding the latter, food trucks are actually the least mobile. Because they are the biggest, they have to deal with parking regulations, have to find parking spots that can fit them, and so forth.

Q: What are the pros and cons of a truck in different seasons?

In the spring and fall, the truck is great. You get to be "outside" every day, meeting great people and giving them instant satisfaction with your great product. People are animated, and the interactions with them are motivating. The weather is usually nice, the breeze feels good, and life is grand!

In the winter, it's pretty different. Everyone is cold, and it's nearly just as cold inside the truck as outside. Many times in the winter, we are just as busy as during the warmer months, but it is much more difficult to move quickly and to be as efficient. So that's definitely frustrating.

The converse is true for the summer. It's so hot and so busy, and the heat makes it difficult to move. Many times inside the truck, we feel like we are gasping for air!

Q: What are situations in which trucks work better than carts and restaurants?

Trucks are just way more efficient than restaurants. They have to be. The goal with the truck is to focus on only a selected few products, to make those products better than anyone else, and then focus all your energy on coming up with the quickest and most efficient system for producing this amazing product over and over again, all day long.

Q: What are some of the features of a restaurant that a truck lacks? Does it limit your menu?

Heat in the winter and air conditioning in the summer! And a bathroom.

Theoretically it doesn't limit our menu since the truck's cooking equipment is all custom and most trucks these days have a separate prep kitchen. The only exception would be for a truck that is totally self-contained, meaning that all the prep and all the equipment cleaning happens inside the truck.

From an equipment standpoint, sometimes trucks can have better equipment than restaurants. This is true first because trucks' menus tend to be smaller since the concepts are usually specialized, and as a result the equipment is completely custom and therefore more efficient at getting the job done. Second, this is true because trucks don't have the same electrical or gas constraints as a restaurant. Everything is either propane or hooked up to the generators. We actually have a conveyer toaster inside our truck that the electrical unit inside the restaurant would not permit!

Q: How does customer service change while working on a truck?

For starters, the customers and customer base changes every day as the truck changes neighborhoods. This is particularly true with new neighborhoods that we have not been to before. Naturally, a truck's customer base is always expanding on a level that's impossible for a restaurant.

In many ways, customer service on the truck must be better than in a restaurant. Truck owners face instant accountability because of Facebook, Twitter, and Instagram photos. Long line today? Everybody will know it within minutes. Messed up someone's order? Rest assured

(continued)

(continued)

there is a photo of the wrong dish somewhere on the Web. So trucks need to be on point every day, all the time. We are under constant scrutiny. It's a bit like a reality show.

Q: What kind of variation in tipping do you see between a truck and a restaurant?

Between a truck and a restaurant with waiter service, there is no comparison. Versus a counter service/take-out restaurant, I would say there is no direct relationship; it varies from truck to truck and restaurant to restaurant. We have found that for our tip jar, three things matter: (1) quality of the food, (2) interacting with customers/good service, and (3) being creative with the design of the tip jar and even writing jokes on it.

Q: What kind of weather benefits a truck, and what kind doesn't? Is there weather that benefits a truck more than a restaurant?

Sunny days, not too hot, not too humid!.

Q: How is advertising different between a truck and a restaurant?

Advertising is part of a truck's DNA. It is an advertising and marketing machine—Twitter, Facebook, Foursquare, and so forth. The trucks live on social media platform. In addition, we get so much media coverage because literally every day we are doing something different, and so we provide media outlets with a good source of content. Restaurants, on the other hand, do the same thing day in and day out, and so they usually get media coverage only when they are "discovered" or once in a while sporadically—like when a magazine goes out to find the best . . . in the city.

Q: Are the employees you hire for a truck different from the ones you would hire for a restaurant? How so?

Yes. First, to work on a truck you need a Mobile Vendors ID Badge. This is a huge pain to get. The city's rules and regulations are such that it takes about three months to get this permission. The process is very confusing as well. So not many people have the permit, and staffing can *be very problematic at times. Many people are interested to work for trucks but cannot because they don't have the permit, and no business or employee can accept a job for three months out into the future. Also, truck employees should be able to drive the truck, should be handy and able to fix things on the fly, need to make lots of decisions on the fly, and they must be okay with working in small spaces.*

Q: Does a truck take more work to operate than a restaurant?

A truck is much more difficult in my opinion, although I know some people might disagree!

Interview 10: Susan Povich of Red Hook Lobster Pound

The Red Hook Lobster Pound was founded by Ralph Gorham and Susan Povich. The company has a storefront in Red Hook, Brooklyn, a food truck in New York City, and two food trucks in Washington, DC. *Inc.* magazine named them one of Brooklyn's top 10 entrepreneurs.

Q: Why did you decide to open a truck?

I started my business in New York City in April 2009. I had a market shop that sold take-out lobster, and I sold lobster rolls at the Brooklyn Flea, so that launched me as a brand. I was used to mobile food in a tent instead of a truck. Then my cousin started a lobster truck with my brand in Washington, DC and had great success, so I decided to open a truck in New York City.

Q: How do you think the public's perception of food trucks has changed over the past five years?

I think that people love food trucks, and our customers especially love them. They're fun, interesting, eye-catching, and have great customer service. But restaurants and police don't like them. There's a misconception that food trucks are freeloaders when the reality is that there

(continued)

(*continued*)

are huge costs involved. Sometimes I feel hated by everyone but my customers.

Q: How did the public initially react to your food truck—was it welcomed, was there an initial excitement?

I was already a brand, so I told writers and bloggers about it. I used momentum from my trucks in Washington and my market shop in New York City.

Q: Where do you foresee the industry going in the next few years?

In New York City, unless they make the legislation more food truck-friendly, the market is going to lose the core people—the smart ones with food backgrounds and unique products—because they won't be able to make money. These people have other options. If the rules prevent them from making money, they're going to close their trucks and go get jobs at law firms or marketing companies. We've already lost a lot of people that way. And when you lose those people, you lose diversity, and all that's left is hot dog stands.

Q: Do you believe that the growth of the industry is sustainable?

Not unless New York City relaxes its antiquated regulations. Soon the only trucks that will be able to afford to stay open will be the ones that are part of a big franchise, like McDonald's or Starbucks. These big companies can afford to lose money on a truck because for them it's just a marketing tool, not a vital source of income.

Q: Where do you see your business going?

I hope our lobbying efforts will pay off and the city will relax its regulations. If not, then maybe Red Hook Lobster Pound can grow by moving out of New York City. I'm not sure if I'm in it for the long haul.

Q: How do you perceive the unity of the industry, as far as competitors working together?

A bunch of the trucks are working together in the New York Food Truck Association, but a lot of people are getting frustrated and exhausted and shutting down. It's hard to bring new people into the Association because not everyone wants to agree to our rules. Trucks in the Association agree to spread out, not park in each other's spots, and be polite. In return, the Association helps truck to build value via rallies and other revenue streams that don't have anything to do with selling food on the street. The Association is also lobbying for better legislation.

Q: How do you feel about food truck lots or festivals?

They're great! Some events are better than others, but they're always worth a try. We recently had a food truck rally that was awesome.

Q: What markets does your food truck target? Are these markets growing?

Red Hook Lobster Pound targets people who will spend money on good food. Often this boils down to people with disposable income, but in Brooklyn, there are some people who will spend their last 20 dollars on a lobster roll! So it's a market that's kind of unique to New York City. Business is growing, in spite of the economy.

Q: Any other words of wisdom?

If you open a new food truck, you will fail unless you have good food. It's all about great products. A unique product is good, but it's not as important as simply having delicious food.

Interview 11: Laura O'Neill of Van Leeuwan Artisan Ice Cream

Van Leeuwen was launched in the spring of 2008 by Ben Van Leeuwen, Laura O'Neill, and Pete Van Leeuwen, serving their own ice cream made using only fresh hormone- and antibiotic-free milk and cream, cane sugars, egg yolks, and the best flavor ingredients from small producers locally and around the world. Van Leeuwen's goal was to bring real, traditionally made, scooped ice cream to the streets of New York City out of beautiful, clean, light-filled trucks. They have since increased their fleet to six

(continued)

(*continued*)

trucks and have added a full coffee and house-made pastry menu to allow year-round vending.

Q: What is the best and worst part of street vending?

The best part: happy customers and working out in the streets beats an office job any day. Worst part: trucks breaking down.

Q: What is the most important lesson you learned since starting vending?

Building a location is very important. It takes time; you can't just try a spot for an hour and expect to gauge its potential. Customers need to be able to count on you being at your location, especially because you're mobile.

Q: What is the best detail you incorporated into the design of your truck?

Easy sliding generator tracks. They make refilling a breeze, and they are super secure.

Q: What would you recommend to an entrepreneur starting out in food trucks?

Never compromise the quality of your product. Use any money you save on overheads to produce a truly awesome product. I would hope that people go in to the food truck business with a passion for food, not just for trends or making money.

Q: What is the full extent of the Van Leeuwen Ice Cream empire right now?

Six trucks, three brick-and-mortar stores, wholesale of pints to grocery stores, wholesale of tubs to restaurants, and in-house bakery operation.

Q: How is running stores different from running trucks?

Stores are a lot of work to start up but can be running smoothly quickly with the right systems in place. Trucks are awesome, but there's a lot that can go wrong. I would say if you have a product that can survive as a store, don't do a truck.

Q: What are your thoughts on carts versus trucks?

In our experience, carts don't have the same allure as trucks. They are also very labor intensive, as you need to tow them into place and then find somewhere to park the car. We have one cart for events but would not street vend with a cart.

Q: How important is wholesale to your overall business?

We take our wholesale seriously, but as there is a middle man (a distributor), it is not our bread and butter at this point. Getting the packaging ready was a lot of work, but now that it's in place, we can expand our number of accounts with very little extra work.

Q: Does being in Whole Foods make it easier to sell on the street?

It's definitely a positive thing for brand recognition. We put our truck on our retail packaging to ensure people make the connection.

Q: How do you stay on top of maintenance for all the trucks?

We do our best to catch issues with the trucks before they get out of control, but the trucks are old, and there are always unforeseen issues. We have log books for oil changes and so forth.

Q: What percentage of your time do you spend overseeing maintenance?

Wow, it feels like all the time! No, really, I'm not sure about a percentage, but issues seem to come in ebbs and flows.

Q: What breaks most often? The truck? Or equipment on the truck?

I'd say the truck, but coffee equipment can be delicate too.

Interview 12: Thomas DeGeest of Wafels & Dinges

Wafels & Dinges was one of the first branded food trucks in New York City. Wafels & Dinges roughly translates into waffles and things. The Wafels truck specializes in wafels and has a broad menu of delicious treats. Thomas runs a food truck, several food carts, and is looking into a brick and mortar store in 2012.

Q: What was your background before Wafels & Dinges?

I actually had zero culinary background or restaurant backgrounds. I worked for big consulting firms like Andersen Consulting and Price Waterhouse Cooper. My last employer was IBM, so I was actually management consultant. That really didn't help me to make wafels. What did help me was the fact that I was from Belgium and that I could kind of consult with myself in the world of Belgian waffle makers. It was easy to get access to the right people. What did help me was that when you start a food truck, it's more than making food; it's running a business. The business aspect helped there.

Q: What are the best and worst parts of working on a food truck?

I was one of the earliest branded food trucks out there (I don't like the term gourmet because a lot of people serve good food). One of the best things is that it's an incredible opportunity being on the truck in the streets of New York. You're catching a lot of eyeballs, and right off the bat, we were very unique when we started out. A truck allows for good branding and a good design, more so than a store sometimes. Another great part is that you can really get to know your markets by moving around, which is huge, because otherwise you'd have to make a $250,000 bet on a store without knowing where your best markets are. The worst part is the unpredictability that comes with navigating so many different stakeholders on the street. It goes from parking regulations to food truck regulations to cops to building owners to more traditional vendors like halal, hot dog, and coffee vendors. You have to navigate all those different stakeholders every day. There are always surprises out there, including all those trucks with your colleagues and *friends. You sometimes bump up against them and have them right next to you. Unpredictability is a big factor. You have to deal with mechanical unpredictability because your main asset, your truck, may break down at any time, which is something we experienced in 2008 when our only truck broke down. We had a very hard time finding new parts for it and almost went out of business.*

Q: What role has branding played on your truck?

You can have two types of businesses: you can have a known brand of businesses where you are basically a commodity like all the hot dog carts or you can start to brand your business. Branding your business is a lot more than just putting a nice logo on your truck or a nice wrap job on your truck. That's not branding in my eyes. In my eyes, branding means that you really think through every single aspect of your interaction with your customers and you determine how to communicate with your customer with every single interaction. That interaction can just be a visual interaction when a customer looks at your staff, it can be a communication interaction when my staff talks to the customer, it can be another visual when the customer looks at the truck from a distance, it can be a social media interaction where a customer looks at our Facebook page or our Twitter page and the tone of voice we use on Twitter. For me, it is very important to drive that identity of being a Belgian company that is full of experience and a degree of excellence that you can't find anywhere else in the country, and at the same time, we're excellent at the high quality of the service we want to do. We don't take ourselves too seriously. We're still just a wafel company and we're still just little, little Belgians from a tiny little country, squeezed between France and Germany. So that is the message and tone I use to permeate everything we do.

Q: How do you communicate with customers, both on the truck and via social media?

You can have a great tone of voice on Twitter, you can have a great tone of voice on Facebook, but if your staff cannot relate to customers . . . I think your staff has to be able to relate to all the types of people that roam around the streets of New York. It goes from hipsters to people who are

(continued)

(continued)

corporate executives, it goes from blue-collar workers to people who are scientific researchers. For the staff, we tried to hire smart people who have a broad range of interests and who are able to relate to other people on many different levels, and that's the most important communication. The reason we are on social media is (a) you are communicating technical information about our location and our specials, things like that, with a very practical purpose, (b) it's also a branding tool because we are sometimes a little bit funny and that sense of humor helps to define the brand, and (c) it's actually much more than a one-way communication; it's in effect a two-way communication. It offers tremendous insight into what customers like and what customers don't like. For instance, when things go wrong, if a customer is upset or disappointed, it's kind of great to read it on Twitter because it can tell me that a certain staff member isn't completely up to our standards as they're doing their job. Those are all great, great reasons to use social media.

Q: What's it like working with both trucks and carts?

Parking regulations make a pretty good chunk of the streets of New York unavailable to street vendors' trucks, and so carts increase our range of access. It's a lot harder to run a cart than to run a truck because you need to have an additional piece of equipment, which is the towing vehicle, most likely one for each one of your carts. We have a towing vehicle for every one of our carts, and we need to maintain and pay insurance and register four additional vehicles. It's a tough and dangerous job to position those carts up to the curb because you have to back up in New York City traffic. There is a lot of negatives to using carts, and I wouldn't necessarily recommend using them to people who don't have the organization and the staff to really make it happen, but the biggest advantage is that you increase your range of access.

Q: What makes your truck distinct?

We are driven by a very strong belief in the importance of design, so what we do is not extremely complicated—it just doesn't happen overnight. The way we've designed our carts, what we've put in terms of graphics on our carts, it happens over many, many weeks of working with a professional design agency. We spent significant effort and money on getting those designs to where we wanted them to be. So, that's the only difference. I see a lot of people wrapping their trucks, which I don't. I don't think it needs to be very complex; I think simplicity goes a long way. At the end of the day, your truck needs to be about the food, not how flashy it looks.

Q: What would your recommendations be for someone wanting to start their own food truck?

I still think there is opportunity for people who want to own a food truck in New York, but you have to get your expectations clear. There are a lot of trucks in the city; there's a lot of competition for spots. You need people who are scouts for new locations; you need to be able to think out of the box and maybe try new locations that are off the beaten path. It may take you time to build those. A food truck can be a great start to build a restaurant business. If you want to stay in the food truck business, you can scale it up to multiple units. The moment you start going to multiple units, you start creating economies of scale. That's when you're going to start seeing some rewards for your work. The other thing is that it is very hard work. It is a 24/7 job as far as I'm concerned, and you have to be able to deal with a lot of unexpected, somewhat stressful events. You have to have a pretty strong stomach; you have to deal with everything on the street. It's not for lighthearted or softhearted people. All these things have to be considered if you want to start a food truck. If you want to do it, and if you have a good concept, everything is possible.

Q: What do you see in the future for Wafels and Dinges? More trucks, carts, a restaurant, or something else?

We are looking at trying a store concept in 2012 in New York City. We're looking at a wafels store. With any wafels in a store, we'd have to be pretty true to the concept; in other words, I don't want a wafel shop that's going to be serving paninis and fruit bowls and what have you; it would have to be wafels and not much else. If the store concept works, our growth as a company will be geared more toward the stores. If it turns out the store in New York becomes a failure, that it's not an option for growth, we're probably going to stay a rather small local player within New York.

Interview 13: Kenny Lao of Rickshaw Dumplings

Rickshaw Dumpling Bar is New York-based Asian, multiunit fast casual dining concept with a focused menu of six types of dumplings, each served with a unique dipping sauce and paired with a noodle soup or entrée salad. The core business of two profitable Manhattan fast casual restaurants is supplemented by a fleet of four mobile food trucks, a kiosk in Times Square, and a future line of frozen dumplings to be sold via national retail outlets. Rickshaw has won a number of accolades including Top 10 Best Street Food in the World, *Travel+Leisure*, Top 20 Food Trucks in the USA, QSR *Weekly*, and Nine Most Eye-Catching Trucks in America, *Elle Décor*.

Q: What are your thoughts on the relationship between street vendors and brick-and-mortar restaurants?

As an owner of a business who had brick-and-mortar restaurants before trucks, I am very sensitive to restaurants who object to mobile vending. The most important thing to remember is that you should not only abide by the rules that govern mobile vending in your city, but you should also be respectful of local businesses. In New York City, there is a rule that you cannot park within 20 feet of any business's doors. We do one better and try not to park on the same block or even on the same side of the street when we can from food businesses that may see us as a threat. That being said, it is important to become an integral part of the fabric of the neighborhood you plan on inhabiting, and just like any good business, you should introduce yourself and your business to the folks who are close to where you park. Get to know the other business owners by name—it makes a difference. There are always business owners who see you as a threat and, in some cases, you may be, but I think that the best thing to do is to make them realize you are a small business as well and just trying to make it.

Q: How much prep/cleanup goes into a service period?

If we open for lunch at 11 AM, we are loading, driving, parking, prepping, and cooking from 8:30 AM onward. It takes about two and a half hours to get all that done, giving ample room for parking and setup. Your shutdown should be about two hours, including shutting down at location, driving back to where you park your truck, and cleaning and restocking.

Q: How do you motivate staff?

I think it is important to pay fairly. This is a tough job to fill, and the people that work your truck will need to not only give great customer service and be able to cook well but also be able to deal with truck breakdowns, parking a large vehicle, maintenance, and the weather. Always thank your staff for a great day, let them keep a tip jar, and overpay.

Q: How have the trucks helped with the Rickshaw brand?

When we opened our first truck, we had one store in the Flatiron District of Manhattan. I would hear people say, "Did you know Rickshaw now has a truck?" When we opened the 45th Street midtown location, we had three trucks, and I heard, "Did you know the Rickshaw truck has a store?" I think the truck, is a great marketing tool and really gets your brand out on the street. For us, dumplings were a natural sell.

Interview 14: Keith Klein of Milk Truck NYC
keithkleincreative.com

Milk Truck is a New York City food truck that specializes in premium grilled cheese sandwiches. Founded by Keith Klein, a former creative director, Milk Truck began operating at a flea market and has grown up into a truck. The concept has received rave reviews from Thrillist, Zagat, Grub Street, UrbanDaddy, and Serious Eats. Accolades include the Milk Truck Classic being ranked #46 of 101 Best Sandwiches List 2010, *New York Magazine*, and winner of 2011 "Big Cheesy" Grilled Cheese Cook Off, *NY Daily News*.

(continued)

(continued)

Q: What was the inspiration for Milk Truck NYC?

The idea for Milk Truck began in the summer of 2009. I was working as a creative director and consultant in advertising, and there was very little paying work around. I had an idea that maybe I could create and execute some sort of business idea as a way to show potential clients how I worked. Effectively, I was hiring myself to create a brand. But what was different is that instead of creating it for a company that was paying me, I was creating it for myself. And if it worked, when I suggested something to a client, it would be based on what I'd done with the brand I'd created. I'd have skin in the game. Plus, deep down, I'd been wanting to make something that I could sell for a while but hadn't really done anything about it. Food was something I'd been interested in for a long time. I'd worked in lots of restaurants earlier in my life, I'd studied at the French Culinary Institute, and I had always cooked. So it seemed like a natural place for me to focus on. Trucks and carts were coming on the scene, and they seemed to be a way in, to create a food brand. I wanted something familiar that could be made better, made into something delicious. The actual idea came to me at about 4 in the morning one sleepless night: grilled cheese. The name came a bit later, by kind of deconstructing what cheese was made up of: milk. We advertising types like that high-concept stuff.

Q: What is the best and worst part of street vending?

Best part of street vending is taking your idea, this ephemeral thing, and after going through the arduous process of actually getting it off the ground, to see people line up to eat the food, your food, is pretty cool.

Worst part: the lack of certainty. The street is a very tricky place. Something is always happening, something that can have an adverse effect on your business for the day, for the week. There's a lot riding on where you park, and that is always a crap shoot because of regulations, the business community, the weather, and the competition.

Q: What is the most important lesson you learned since starting vending?

Two things: One, that you should be able to prepare the food you are selling quickly. It is a fast-service concept, not a restaurant. There is a threshold on how long people will wait, and weather will radically change that threshold. And two, that you have to adapt. Things happen. Every day. And either you adapt or you fold up and go home. If you can't stomach surpise and uncertainty, you really shouldn't be in this business.

Q: What is the best detail you incorporated into the design of your truck?

For us, there were a couple of things. We sell grilled cheese sandwiches and milk shakes, items that people are familiar with. But our brand is called Milk Truck, which doesn't exactly shout out what we sell, so we wrapped text around the middle of the truck with our menu items large enough to telegraph what we were about. Then we made our name really big and put it on the side.

Q: What would you recommend to an entrepreneur starting out in food trucks?

Study food trends, and have a concept that is a fresh take on something familiar, either by mashing two cultures together or finding a new way to express something. Keep your food costs in mind while you're creating it, and be sure that you can execute it quickly and consistently.

Q: How important is a clear brand identity in the food truck market?

Super important. People like to put food in generic categories—the dumpling truck, the Korean taco truck, the grilled cheese truck, etc. With a strong brand, you can build a barrier to competition and inspire loyalty, as long as you are selling something delicious and you are nice about it.

Q: What should people think about when developing a brand?

People don't want to work too hard to figure out what you are selling. The name should give them a pretty good idea of what kind of product you have on board. Every design element, from font to logo to color scheme are cues to what kind of brand you are. Loud, quiet, upscale, authentic, modern, real, hip, etc. Be consistent in your message with these.

(continued)

(continued)

Q: What are the key ways to convey brand (truck design, website, social media)?

Design is fun and cool, and it's often all we focus on. And it is super important for your brand to have a great design that reflects what you sell and who you are and does so consistently across your truck, your website, and the various mediums, social and otherwise. But there are dozens of points of contacts with your customers, and they all convey your brand message. How do you answer the phone, what kind of people work for you, how do they talk to customers, how clean your trucks are, etc.? These are the things that show the philosophy behind the brand, or the lack thereof.

Q: What guidance should entrepreneurs be prepared to offer graphic designers?

Be very clear about what you are trying to convey, strategically and philosophically. Give them clear parameters about what kind of food you are selling, why you believe in it, and what you want to say. Then let them do their job. We hire designers because they speak in a language we don't. If we are clear about our message, a good designer will find a coherent, logical, visually interesting way to convey it.

Q: What sorts of mistakes do you see other entrepreneurs making in their truck branding?

Their name not conveying clearly what they sell, not having design curb appeal, not being visible on the street, emulating other truck's designs rather than having their vision of what they want to do, chasing trends, puns. Puns are really bad.

Q: Do you do brand consulting? If so, what is the best way to get in touch with you?

I do do brand consulting for all sorts of businesses, from luxury brands to automobiles to food concepts. And with the latter, I can safely say that any suggestion or idea I have is one that comes from experience.

Interview 15: Tim Volkema of Kasa Indian

Kasa Indian was cofounded by Anamika Khanna and Tim Volkema. Kasa introduces its customers to the way Indians eat at home—Indian food made from scratch. Each dish honors centuries-old cooking traditions. At Kasa you'll get delicious meals made from natural, local ingredients as well as specialty spices imported from India. Kasa operates a fast casual restaurant and two food trucks in San Francisco.

Q: What is the best and worst part of operating a food truck?

Best: feeling like a rock star driving the truck around—lots of waves, head nods, thumbs-ups, and stares. People are really into our truck design and always appear to be excited to see it rolling around town. Also, getting to serve Indian street food on real San Francisco streets is amazing! Kasa has always served the kati roll, which is a classic street food item from India, so it makes a nice circle to be serving kati rolls to San Franciscans this way. Finally, the mobility is a gift. There are many places where it wouldn't make sense to open a Kasa restaurant, but there are enough customers to support a food truck service. That gives us access to customers that may never otherwise experience Kasa.

Worst: breakdowns and overly complex permitting processes.

Q: What is the most important lesson you learned about your concept since you started your food truck?

Kasa is great lunch food! Our restaurant is in a residential neighborhood, so dinner has always been the busier meal because the neighborhood is much more active at night. The food truck allowed us to confirm that Kasa's kati rolls work really well for lunch in busy noon-time markets.

Q: What is the best detail you incorporate into the design of your truck?

We have a phrase on the back of our truck that reads, "Horn OK Please." This was a nod to India and its many, many trucks. If you've ever visited India, it would be hard to miss this phrase painted colorfully on

(continued)

(continued)

most trucks and commercial vehicles. There are several theories on its origin, so I'll leave it to your curiosity and Wikipedia to sort out which one makes the most sense. We thought it was a fun detail, and our Indian customers love it.

Q: What would you recommend to an entrepreneur starting out in food trucks?

Develop a dead simple concept that can be easily understood. Specialization is key, and make sure the name of your truck clearly conveys what you will be serving your customers. Avoid generalities like "California Cuisine Truck." Also, increase whatever your start-up budget figure is by 50%. You'll need it for repairs, staff training, and many other unforeseen costs.

Q: How does the food truck fit into your hospitality concept?

The truck plays two key roles for us: new distribution opportunities and brand building. First, it allows us to access and test many areas that work for trucks, only some of which may eventually be viable brick-and-mortar locations. Second, we have a "Visit Our Restaurant" message on our truck design, so customers know where to find our permanent location in the SF's Castro neighborhood. We have seen in-store traffic pick up after we launched the truck.

Q : What is the most challenging management issue pertaining to the truck operations?

Trucks require high caliber, trustworthy managers. Running a truck requires an ability to solve problems quickly on the fly. You do not have the resources of a full restaurant at your disposal but are expected to create a similar customer experience. Also, each service is different depending on the location, so it takes more planning than a restaurant that operates the same location every day. It should be noted that the majority of truck sales are in cash, and that opens up numerous theft opportunities. It is critical to have a manager with an extremely high level of personal integrity.

Q: How do you stay on top of maintenance issues?

We have a shared Google calendar to which all our truck staff members have access. Each maintenance activity is scheduled at the appropriate frequency, and the calendar is followed carefully.

Q: How much of your business is street vending versus lots or public events versus private/catered events?

We have one truck dedicated almost 100 percent to street vending, and the other truck is about a 50/50 mix of street vending and private events. Our street vending is 80 percent public and 20 percent private. San Francisco as a whole is probably split 75-25 between vending on public property versus private in favor of public (including city parks).

Q: What is in the future for Kasa fans?

We like the restaurant–truck combo business, so look for a second Kasa store and possibly a third food truck within the next year.

Notes

1. http://articles.latimes.com/2011/may/08/business/la-fi-food-trucks-20110508
2. www.restaurant.org/research/forecast/
3. www.theatlanticcities.com/arts-and-lifestyle/2011/10/food-truck
   -industrial-complex/331/
4. www.technomic.com/_files/Newsletters/Marketbrief/Marketbrief_201008
   .pdf
5. http://marcussamuelsson.com/news/the-wondrous-world-of-street-food
6. www.sidewalksofny.com/index.php/food-truk-tours
7. http://inventors.about.com/library/inventors/blchuckwagon.htm
8. http://lonehand.com/chuckwagon_central.htm
9. http://americanchuckwagon.org/chuck-wagon-history.html
10. www.tablematters.com/index.php/philly-sections/st/sttoms
11. www.barrypopik.com/index.php/new_york_city/entry/lunch_wagon/
12. http://media.wgnradio.com/media/mp3file/2010-01/51777191.mp3
13. www2.macleans.ca/2010/09/30/construction-guys/
14. http://mashable.com/2011/08/04/food-truck-history-infographic/
15. www.qsrweb.com/article/181549/NRA-2011-Food-Truck-Spot-doubles
   -from-inaugural-year
16. http://mobile-cuisine.com/off-the-wire/the-knot-unveils-top-11
   -wedding-trends-for-2011-food-trucks-included/
17. www.nytimes.com/2011/07/17/sunday-review/17foodtrucks.html?_r=1

18. Linda A. Hill, "Becoming the Boss," January 1, 2007, http://hbr.org/product/becoming-the-boss/an/R0701D-PDF-ENG

19. Cameron Hawkins and Associates, "City of Toronto: Review of Toronto a la Cart Pilot Project," April 4, 2011, www.google.com/url?sa=t&rct=j&q=&esrc=s&source=web&cd=1&ved=0CB8QFjAA&url=http%3A%2F%2Fwww.toronto.ca%2Flegdocs%2Fmmis%2F2011%2Fex%2Fbgrd%2Fbackgroundfile-37419.pdf&ei=Pqy6Tv7eJoXZ0QGIzozfCQ&usg=AFQjCNHid7CvPo36MPy4VzG5KsDtSG4GSw

20. Marcus Gee, "Taking Street Food from Flop to Fame," *The Globe and Mail*, November 4, 2011, www.theglobeandmail.com/news/national/toronto/marcus-gee/taking-street-food-from-flop-to-fame/article2226549/

21. www.pbs.org/wnet/need-to-know/five-things/starting-your-own-food-truck/4268/

22. www.quora.com/Food-Trucks/What-is-the-average-daily-revenue-for-food-trucks

About the Author

DAVID WEBER is the founder and president of the New York City Food Truck Association (NYCFTA), which brings together small businesses that own and operate premium food trucks in New York City. The Association is focused on the issues of innovation in hospitality, high-quality food, and community development. Through his work at the NYCFTA, David liaises with local governments and communities throughout New York City in order to help reinvent food truck vending in a way that is beneficial to the city, food truck entrepreneurs, and New Yorkers. David is also a cofounder of Rickshaw Dumplings, a growing fast casual chain of two restaurants, four food trucks, and a kiosk in Times Square. Prior to his experience in hospitality, David was a technology and business consultant. He holds an MBA from New York University's Stern School of Business and a BA in English Literature from Yale University. David can be reached at: david@nycfoodtrucks.org or david@foodtrucker.info.

Index